Learning from the Children

Learning from the Children

REFLECTING ON TEACHING

Cindylee Villareale

www.redleafpress.org
800-423-8309

ℐℨⅼⅼⅼⅼℐⅼℨX

Published by Redleaf Press
10 Yorkton Court
St. Paul, MN 55117
www.redleafpress.org

First edition 2009
Cover design by Jim Handrigan
Cover photograph by Cindylee Villareale
Interior typeset in Berkeley Oldstyle Medium and designed by Erin New
Interior photos by Cindylee Villareale; Kim Street, who took the photos
    on pages 3, 11, 32, 38, 43, 60, 75, and 91; and Jim Handrigan, who took
    the photos on pages 19 and 96
Developmental edit by Deanne Kells
Printed in the United States of America
16   15   14   13   12   11   10   09   1   2   3   4   5   6   7   8

Library of Congress Cataloging-in-Publication Data
Villareale, Cindylee.
    Learning from the children : reflecting on teaching / Cindylee Villareale.
    — 1st ed.
       p. cm.
    Includes bibliographical references.
    ISBN 978-1-933653-71-6
1. Teaching—Vocational guidance. 2. Teachers—Conduct of life. I. Title.
    LB1775.V49 2009
    371.1'0023—dc22
                                        2008032784

Printed on FSC certified paper

371.10023
.V55
2009

FSC
Mixed Sources
Product group from well-managed
forests and other controlled sources

Cert no. SW-COC-002283
www.fsc.org
© 1996 Forest Stewardship Council

This book is dedicated to my sister, Marci Randi. You are a "unique." Your beauty, inside and out, is mesmerizing. I have watched you and admired you my whole life, and because of your bravery, I am free to be me—my own unique self.
You helped me see the value of the stories. Thanks for giving me time to breathe.

Learning from the Children

Acknowledgments

To Pete, Levi, and Jason: Thank you for giving me the gift of time to write. Without the time, this would all just still be in my head.

To Mom: I inherited my ability to see people, really see them, from you. I am blessed to be your child, both in my youth and in our old age.

To Monica, Lavina, and Don: Thanks for keeping me on track.

To Kevin, Steve, Rebecca, and Taylor: Thanks for your encouragement.

To Jack and Ava, who have some stories told in this book: You helped me to see the value of a preschool teacher.

To Catherine Banas: Thanks for providing your professional input and advice.

To Kim Street: Thanks for your amazing photography and support.

To Redleaf Press; Kyra Ostendorf, the acquisitions editor; and Deanne Kells, the developmental editor: Thanks for helping my dream come true.

And finally, thanks to the One who gave me the wisdom and the words.

Introduction

The children who were in my first preschool class celebrate their twenty-first birthdays this year. I wonder what they have learned since I last saw them. Has what they learned in my class had any effect on who they are and where they are? Many researchers have tried to answer that question. If you work in the early learning field for very long, you will be able to quote a few of their findings. It is those quotes that we bury in our minds and hearts to remind us of why we spend our days tying shoes, counting to twenty, and singing "The Itsy Bitsy Spider" with so much zeal that you'd think it was the first time our fingers had ever climbed that water spout. But within my wonderings of where those students are now is an introspective question: Where am I?

I believe that every person you encounter can teach you something. Each person can give you a new perspective—a look into life that you would miss if you had not met that person. If this is true, then my life's education has relied mostly on four-year-olds. I have paid for many college courses; read bookshelves of books, research reports, and journals; and been intrigued by many speakers. But the four-year-olds gave me an education that doesn't always come from books. While they grew before my eyes and called me "Teacher," quite often I was the one who received the gift of learning.

So, even as those now-twenty-one-year-olds are out forging their way in the world, I want to share some of the stories and gifts of learning that they and later students gave me. Each year I used those gifts with the next class, who in turn brought me a new set of gifts. I hope these stories will become gifts for you to use as well.

A Note about the Organization of the Book

Because the stories of my experiences with the children are the core part of the learning I want to pass on, I begin each chapter with a story. These are true stories that I was blessed to be a part of. I wrote them in the present tense, so that you might feel the power of being there, in the moment, with the children and me.

After telling each story, I share my own personal responses to it. I want you to understand the impact these encounters had on me as a person and as an educator. Starting with my personal perspective, I move outward to generalize lessons that everyone who knows the story might learn from it. Finally, I ask you to reflect on the story's impact for you, at whatever point you are in your own life. In a sense, I want you to own the story—to learn from it in your own unique way.

I hope you enjoy the book and find it helpful. I know there are stories inside of you too. Don't forget to pass them on!

PART ONE

Be Your Best for Me

1

Ava's Song

In my child care center we have one room that is long and narrow. It has several uses, but we always use it as the nap room. The children sleep on thick mats with crib sheets, and they have their favorite sleeping necessities. Ava, the youngest three-year-old, always has her blanket, her special baby-sized satin pillow, and one small beanbag animal. Today she has a black dog. The music from our favorite naptime tape is drifting through the room.

"Cindy, Cindy." I look toward the other end of the room. Ava is sitting up on her nap mat. I had thought she was asleep when I checked ten minutes ago. My first instinct is to tell her to lie back down and go to sleep. I am writing a plan for next week and do not want to interrupt my thought process. She always follows my instructions; this time she would have complied as well. But then I remind myself of my earlier vow to be *present and available*. I hit the save key and go to her side.

"Will you rock?" she inquires. Rocking with Ava means cuddling with her and all her naptime items in our classroom rocker. I feel extremely pressured to get my planning completed; I know that if I take time to rock with Ava, I will not finish my paperwork before the others awake. This will start a snowball of pressure and stress, ending with staying late and being less present for my own children. When I look at Ava's tender eyes, though, I know that this is more than an attempt to put off sleep.

Ava grabs up everything, and I easily swoop her into my arms. We work our way into a comfortable position, rocking to the slow sounds of a tenor sax harmonized by the purring of ocean waves. Ava begins to sing, "Twinkle, twinkle little star . . ." Again I am tempted to hush her to sleep. "No, let the moment happen," I constrain myself. I stay quiet. She has a perfect singing voice. At age three, she sings more sweetly than the birds.

Completing the last line, she asks, "Why did you let me sing?" "Why . . . ?" is a common question in my classroom, and it is always followed by a meaningful answer. So I answer.

"Because you seemed like you needed to sing. Sometimes it helps us feel more relaxed and happy when we sing." My reply even surprises me. "Your singing makes me feel good inside too." She gently smiles and repeats the serenade.

"Okay, now I can sleep." She crawls down, goes back to her mat, and is asleep before I can clear my eyes enough to type.

It is a naptime ritual now—we rock, and she sings. I find that her voice is a peaceful means to refresh my soul in the middle of the day. We have had a series of conversations about how music touches our hearts and how sharing music touches our world. Someday, her voice will touch the world outside our walls.

Be Present and Available

It was a real struggle for me to put down my work and take time for Ava. I don't have planning time outside of the classroom. There is no other time for planning, and I pride myself on my lesson plans. It takes thorough planning to be effective as an educator. Every week I have classroom goals as well as individual goals. So I needed to concentrate and focus. I was on a thought train, and I didn't really want to derail it. It would have been so easy just to tell Ava to lie down and rest so I could continue with my planning.

After that time with Ava, I realized that vowing to be present and available for the children was going to take some practice. How many times even that same day had I put off a child so that we could complete my agenda? Right before naptime Karrin had asked to show me something, and I had told her that we would look at it later. But I hadn't followed through. Now I was wondering what I had missed. Teachable moments have passed me by.

Spencer Johnson wrote an amazing book about being present in the present. This is one of my favorite quotes from it:

> *Being In The Present Means*
> *Tuning Out Distractions*
> *And Paying Attention To*
> *What Is Important, Now.*
> *You Create Your Own Present*
> *By What You Give*
> *Your Attention To Today.*
>
> (Johnson 2003, 40)

The closing lines are powerful: "You create your own present by what you give your attention to today." That sentence works with both definitions of "present." You make a gift out of what you focus your attention on, as well as create your own awareness out of where you choose to direct your attention.

We give children a gift—a present—of being present. This means not just being physically in the room but being available to answer questions and to meet needs, to put their agendas before our own. Ava needed some personal attention. It was not her normal behavior to avoid sleep. Some children keep interrupting in order to avoid napping. That was not the case in this situation. She just needed some special TLC. When I met her needs, she felt comforted and able to sleep.

When you are accessible, your attention and awareness are focused on the children. They must be your first priority—not only in theory, but in action. It is very easy to get caught up in routines and daily activities. There are ever-increasing demands on a teacher's time, and it is easy to get lost in the task rather than be aware of the moment. Multitasking becomes a matter of survival. We must multitask: even when we are talking with a small group of children, we need to be aware of the rest of the children in the room.

I remember the results of one tunnel vision moment I experienced. I was sitting with a child who was having an emotional moment because his friend wouldn't play with him. He was distraught as the friend went off to a different activity that was not what he wanted to do at that moment. So he felt abandoned and betrayed. While I was helping him work through his feelings, a group of girls decided to play beauty shop with a pair of art scissors. Now, I like scissors that work well on paper; I think it eliminates some of the frustration of learning to cut. There is nothing worse then trying to cut paper with dull scissors that don't work. Little hands are just learning to cut, so the scissors need to work well. But if scissors are sharp enough to cut paper easily, they will also cut hair.

The girls had seated Hannah in a chair, wrapped an art shirt around her to look like a smock in the beauty shop, and begun to cut. They lifted her long, brown, glossy hair into the air and snipped it about two inches from the scalp. Several locks had met their demise before I looked up and screamed. The girls immediately began to cry. I have always wondered why they cried—whether it was because I screamed or because they knew what they were doing was wrong. Either way, I joined the crying. Soon the boys joined in, because if Teacher is crying, something must really be wrong. I felt awful. How could I have let this happen? I figured the parents would be irate. I had let them down; I didn't protect their daughter from the Preschool Beauty Salon. The director was walking down the hall when she heard the wailing. But she didn't cry at the sight. She laughed! Now the kids were really confused.

Tunnel vision is not a good idea—really not a good idea. But children are too valuable to be the objects of multitasking. So where is the balance? I have learned a few tricks of the trade over the years. If I am the sole teacher in the room, I never sit on the floor if I cannot see the whole group. Someone needs to have a constant view of the classroom as a whole. When I am team teaching, we use a tool I call "One Up, One Down." This simply means one person can be one-on-one with a child while the other has the responsibility of viewing the group as a whole. But when I am alone, I sit in a chair with a child who needs me, so that I can be eye-to-eye with the child yet still see the whole room.

There are times when a child needs to be the sole owner of your attention. This child has something important to tell you—something so important that you need to stop multitasking and give him or her your attention, while remaining aware of the whole group. How you know the difference is determined by your awareness of the child's needs. In fact, you will see a common thread on every page of this book as you read. This thread is *relationship*. How well you know the individual needs, preferences, talents, and abilities of the children in your class will determine how effective you are as an educator. When you know the tendencies of the children you work with, you will know if a child really needs your attention or is just trying to get help in finding the missing puzzle piece. Even if the latter is the case, taking a moment to look a child in the eye and give him or her your undivided attention will not take long— thirty seconds, tops. That thirty-second moment may be the only time an adult listens to that child the whole day. When I first started teaching, I only made about six cents every thirty seconds. Six cents. It was only six cents for me, but to the child it was priceless.

One quick way to determine if you are multitasking with children is to notice where your eyes are. When a child is talking to you, are you looking at him or checking in the teacher cabinet for a colored marker?

Wherever your eyes are looking, that is where you will find your primary attention focused.

Being present and available for the children is tough. Teachers' minds have so much to focus on: what is being said, what kind of play is happening, parents coming in, other staff in the room, where the missing shoe is, parents' concerns from last night, how to get the picky child to eat lunch, how to get the rambunctious child to rest, how to approach the parents of a child we have concerns about, the individual needs of the children . . . The list goes on. Then, of course, we have to teach.

No wonder some people are amazed at what we do. Now that I write it down, *I* am amazed. But we do it, and usually we do it well. And when the child who sits up on her mat in the middle of naptime wants to rock, we rock. We put down the planning, we put down the pen, and we are serenaded by the sweet, perfect song of an angel. The serenade fills our hearts with energy to love again. The serenade lifts our spirits so our faces glow with delight again. We breathe in deeply, deep enough to exhale the discouragement so we can breathe in optimism. We wipe away the tears of gratitude, and we get ready for it all to happen again.

Reflection

I remember the tears of that day very clearly. I had found that teachable moment. Not only had I met Ava's needs so that she could rest, but together we opened a door in her life—a door that could lead to a love for and a life filled with music. Not only did her little song affect her, allowing her to feel inner peace, but she knew that her musical gift had touched me. She saw and felt the power of music. What an honor to be the one who broadened her views and enhanced her life. I gave her my present, and that gift may have changed a life. In fact, make that two lives. Once I had a taste of being present and aware, I was addicted.

There was no going back; it was too powerful. This moment changed my life and was the beginning of many new presents.

Moments like these develop strong relationships. My willingness to value Ava as a person by giving her my attention increased her own self-value. Many great theories and studies discuss how relationships affect development. Urie Bronfenbrenner's book *The Ecology of Human Development* (1979) emphasizes social and cultural influences on a child's development. He states that all relationships and social experiences have an impact on a child's growth. He breaks up a child's world into four systems or circles. The closer the system, the greater the effect on the child. The closest circle is the microsystem. It is where children spend most of their time: at home, in school, and in their neighborhood. This inner circle has the greatest potential to affect a child. You are in that circle.

So what present do you want to give the children in your class? In a teacher's day there is so much to do. Every day, researchers bless us with one more thing to add to that list to make the perfect, high-quality early learning environment. But what can you do today to give the children the gift of being present—aware of them and their needs? If you watch, they will show you.

Keep a Vow to Be Present and Available

1. Purposefully listen to children. Check your eye contact.
2. Make yourself available by walking around the room until children speak with you first. If you are busy, they may not feel they can interrupt.
3. Tell children, "I am here if you need me." We sometimes just assume they know this, but they often don't. It is comforting for them to hear it, and saying it reminds us to do it.

Suggested Reading

Burman, Lisa. 2008. *Are you listening? Fostering conversations that help young children learn.* Saint Paul: Redleaf Press.

Johnson, Spencer, M.D. 2003. *The present: The gift that makes you happy and successful at work and in life.* New York: Doubleday.

2

One with Pinkeye

One with pinkeye, one just finishing the flu, and one child with a temperature of 102.2°. I feel used, creatively drained, unappreciated, and—most of all—tired. But tomorrow will begin my twelve-days-of-Christmas vacation. So, for about the millionth time today, I put on a smile, hug the child, and look up another parent's phone number. The vision of spending my break with two gooey red eyes while throwing up and having a fever is only allowed a brief stop in my brain before I give it a swift kick.

The cherished time-to-go-home arrives. Shoes need to be found and put on, parent communication is imperative, and proper salutations need delivering. As parents arrive, the bad news of illness is distributed. One dad, on his way out, reminds Jack that he will not see me until after Christmas. Jack understands that this is a requirement to give a Merry Christmas wish. He turns my way and proclaims, "Merry Christmas, Cindy, and I love you." I let his words penetrate my heart and use them as a shield to keep doubt away. I send the wish, with love, back to him. We are a room apart, but he has hugged me with his words, and I hug him back. Jack, in that moment of time, renews my calling. His declaration of love is my reminder to enjoy my twelve-days-of-Christmas break, but then to come back and smile some more.

Be Ready to Give of Yourself

Sometimes they are the only reward we get—the words of a child—and that reward is far greater than any Oscar or Emmy. Drawing your strength from your relationship with the children is imperative for long-term survival. Children are the reason we do what we do. They are so valuable that we can risk pinkeye on our Christmas break.

Whatever your work environment, children are the number one priority. All else takes a back seat, sometimes even to our own detriment. Most of the people I have met in this field are very dedicated to the well-being of children and are heroes for it, and I have seen many of these heroes burn out. Just before my twelve-days-of-Christmas holiday, I wasn't at a state of burnout; I just needed a break. When I was teaching, I had wise mentors and supervisors who taught me how to draw strength from my relationships with those I was working so hard to serve. They taught me how to watch for the signs of burnout and how to regenerate before I even got close. Later in my career, however, as a center director, I did not have those supports in place.

I loved my job, my center, the families I served, and the staff who served alongside me. There were so many details to attend to, and I worked long hours. The children who came to our center deserved the best, and it was my job to make sure that every single one of them got it. The place was a mess when I was hired on. It had lacked leadership for some time. The sub-director was doing her best to mop it all up, but there was a lot of dirt around. Most of the staff needed to be replaced or retrained. After a while, even those who needed retraining decided that my standards were higher than they wanted to reach, so they left on their own. Those who stayed eventually became part of management in the company. The facility required cleanup and repairs. Family relationships needed to be built back and trust reestablished. Programs needed adjustment, and enrollment had to be increased. To top it all off, I was committed to getting the program accredited by the National Association for the Education of Young Children (NAEYC).

We achieved all of these goals within two years. For those two years I worked between fifty and sixty hours a week. But the progress was incredible! We were accredited. I had one of the highest parent satisfaction ratings in the company, our enrollment had grown, and staff turnover was down by more than half. Because I loved my job, my center, the families I served, and the staff who served alongside me, I kept going.

There were warning signs along the way. But I either didn't see them or didn't want to see them. I got sick—really sick. My personal relationships were suffering. My family was suffering. I hardly knew what was going on in my own children's lives. In fact, I think I knew more about my staff's lives than I did about my sons'.

Then it happened. I didn't care anymore if the paperwork wasn't perfect. I tried to cut back my hours, but they needed me there—or at least I thought they did. I dreaded going to work in the morning. I was tired all the time. I dressed more comfortably. I looked less professional, even wearing less and less makeup. People commented that I looked tired, so I just drank more caffeine. I couldn't concentrate. I made more mistakes. My patience wore thin. I forgot my basic responsibilities. The staff complained—most of them didn't complain to me, but I knew. Then I got sick again. Eventually, I just gave up.

Burnout is exactly what it sounds like. You burn out all of your energies, your drive, your desire to even be there. It is most readily apparent in the person who just doesn't care anymore. People in a burnout state have used up all the energy they have to give. They have given out all that they have without refilling their supply; it has been a process of all give and no get.

It is important to have an anti-burnout plan. This is a plan to refill your "give tank" on a regular basis without letting the tank get too low.

I tell my son, who just bought his first car, that he should not let his gas tank get below the half-full line. It is better for the car and better for his mother's peace of mind. It is so easy to get caught up in the excitement of teenage life and forget to check the gas gauge. In Minnesota, especially in the winter, running out of gas can leave you cold and abandoned on the side of the road. Allowing your "give tank" to get too low could have a similar effect.

So what fills a tank? Many things. First of all is proper health, the basic necessities of life. Make sure you get sufficient rest, exercise, and nutrition. I used to roll my eyes at that statement because we hear that advice everywhere we go. Even late-night television has infomercials that will tell you how important those things are. But now I am older and sound like an infomercial myself. Get rest; eat right; exercise!

Now the more fun stuff—have fun! In your classroom, during the flow of the day, make sure you are having fun. Laugh with the children, play with the children, paint with them, run with them, and make snowmen with them. Whatever it is that you enjoy, do it. Some of my favorite memories over the past twenty years are of times when I was playing with children.

Filling your tank with fun is different for everyone, but for me it involves doing something totally crazy. For example, when I worked in an all-day program, we were spending our last few weeks in our building before we moved to a new center. The old, decrepit building was to be torn down and the empty area paved for a parking lot. We were studying soil at the time, which was during Oregon's ninety-degree summer. So we dug up the grass in a huge circle, fluffed up the dirt, and added water. We had a two-foot-deep mud hole. It was great. The neighborhood came out to watch, and our story made the newspapers. Great times, great fun—tank refilled!

There are lots of tank fillers. For example, I always choose music for naptime that is my personal favorite—but still appropriate for children. Playing the same naptime music every day helps the children to rest better. They aren't tuning into the music to see what is next because they have heard it all before. So since you have the same music playing day after day, it is important that you like it.

Other tank fillers? There are many: recognizing your successes, helping someone in need, going beyond the call of duty, giving a grateful hug, sending a note of encouragement to fill someone else's tank, refreshing your senses. I used to keep air fresheners around just to have a breath of fresh air. Some rooms can get pretty stuffy!

You may not know what will fill your give tank. If you are a beginning teacher, you may not know what will fill your tank *or* what will draw from it. It won't take long for you to find out, however. The first time you have an upset parent, you will know exactly what I am talking about. When you walk away from that parent and back to a group of children who need your attention, having to switch modes as quickly as flipping a light switch, you will know that your tank is being drawn from. And that's okay; just don't let it get below the half-full line. If you can, keep it full.

When I had great moments like the one I shared with Jack, I always wrote them down. Having a written record for future reference is a great tank filler. Unfortunately, when we are in the midst of trying situations, children do not often send us words of love and appreciation. Yet it is precisely at those times that you need to remember the wonderful slow-motion moments. If they are not written down and handy, you may find it hard to recall them. The stress of the circumstances may overshadow yesterday's moments of success.

I even went one step further and put my moments in a scrapbook that I kept in my classroom. Parents would ask about the book or just pick it up as they were exploring the room. It was a testament to my commitment and a tribute to our classroom relationships. Children and parents would spend time reading about the great moments in our class and how much I appreciated them. I know: this adds one more thing to do on your ever-growing list, but I promise that this one is well worth your time.

People often ask me why there is such a big turnover of staff in early childhood education facilities. Some teachers realize after they start that it is just not for them. Some can't survive on the paychecks. Some leave for the same reasons people leave all jobs. And some burn out. All the rest of us are lifers: we are in this for life. If you are a lifer, you had better make sure that you have some precautions in place. I tried burnout. It is a disabling syndrome, and it truly burns; it burns badly. It took three months of not working before I felt that I could function normally again. I think I slept most of the first month. It was the end of the second month before I could carry on an intelligent conversation with complete thoughts. At about this same time, I could finally go from one room to another and remember why I had gone there. And somewhere around the end of the third month, I actually began to enjoy children again— maybe not adults yet, but children.

If I close my eyes and listen hard enough, I can still hear Jack's Christmas wish. I can still feel the hug he sent me. Fortunately, there have been many other huggable moments since then. I remember them, and now they get me up and send me to work with my tank full and ready to give.

Reflection

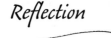

During the time of my Christmas encounter with Jack, I was questioning why I was doing what I was doing. There are days when it feels as if all we are doing is wiping noses. Our plans don't get done. Parents aren't happy. Children aren't happy. We aren't happy. This was one of those days. Jack reminded me that even when we are wiping noses, we are loving, nurturing, and teaching children. Have you ever had your face touched? It is an endearing, tender moment. Skin-to-skin contact provides a connection, a very personal connection. So now, with every nose I wipe, I get down low, look the child right in the eyes, and we remind each other how much we care.

Jeff Johnson has written an excellent book that faces the issue of burnout for early childhood professionals. In *Finding Your Smile Again,* he gives a perfect definition of "burnout": "The term *burnout* was probably imported from the field of electrical engineering. When electrical components are forced to handle too much current, they overheat and burn out. A burned-out light bulb is no longer part of the electrical circuit to which it is connected . . . The bulb no longer gives off light." He goes on to say, "It's the same with people. We burn out, and our light dims; our motors seize, and our energy stops flowing" (Johnson 2007, 14–15).

As care providers we are continuously in tune with people around us. We are empathetic to their feelings and needs, and we see it as our priority to meet those needs. The needs never quit coming. We serve parents, and we serve communities. The needs seem endless, and we can take on more and more, whether physically or emotionally, until—pop!—our circuit overloads, and we blow a fuse or burn out our light bulb.

In what ways can you guard against burning out your light bulb? Do you have a meter that registers your tank level? You are responsible for creating your own anti-burnout system. So what are you going to do?

Practical Ways to Avoid Burnout

1. Make a list of what fills your tank. Post it inside a cupboard so you can look at it when you are getting tired. This will remind you to get a refill.
2. Look over your plan for this week, and find one activity that will fill your tank. Highlight it, and don't forget to have fun with it. Taking this opportunity once a day is even better.
3. Ask a teammate to join you in completing the Burnout Assessment Questionnaire (see appendix A). If possible, give one to your supervisor, and ask him or her to hand out this questionnaire regularly.

Suggested Reading

Johnson, Jeff A. 2007. *Finding your smile again: A child care professional's guide to reducing stress and avoiding burnout.* Saint Paul: Redleaf Press.

3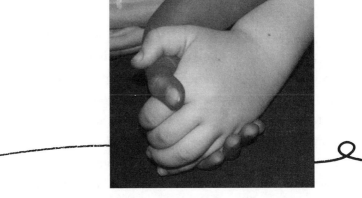

The Hand-Holding Wait Line

I am the sole caretaker in a room of ten preschoolers. Having patience is a matter of sheer survival. I often get interrupted by a child who needs my attention while I am talking with a parent. It is rude to the parent to interrupt and unfair to the child to give him or her only half of my attention, so I use what I call the Hand-Holding Wait Line. When I am speaking with someone and a child needs my attention, the child is to walk up and hold my hand rather than interrupt. This assures the children that they are next to get my undivided attention, while I am allowed to finish my conversation.

Usually a child walks up and starts talking, not noticing that I am busy. I offer the child my hand. The child knows what it means and begins the Hand-Holding Wait Line. If a second child needs me and I am still involved in a conversation, that child can hold the other hand of the child who is holding mine. This makes a line of those who are next for my attention. I use the hand-holding line not only when speaking with parents but when talking with children as well. It teaches them to be patient, and it gives them the assurance that when it is their turn, I will listen with both ears. I try not to make the wait too long; I want to honor their patience and their limits. There was one morning when it got a little out of hand.

Carlie's mom and I are discussing the upcoming winter holiday party. It is early in the day, and children are still arriving. A "good morning" greeting is exchanged as each child arrives and parents leave. Ralynn is the first in the room. She immediately runs over with wonder in her eyes and starts to tell me about her adventures with the new snow outside. I hold out my hand, and she graciously grabs on and begins the patience-practicing Hand-Holding Wait Line. The mom and I continue with our conversation, and I notice a second child walk up to say something about our luck in getting new snow. But Ralynn knows the drill and offers him her hand so that he begins to practice patience as well. I feel pretty proud. We are in a part of Washington state that does not get snow very often; it is an exciting topic.

My conversation with the mom ends a good ten minutes later. I usually would not let a child wait that long, but I had lost track of time. As I begin looking at the first child, I start laughing. All eight of the children are holding hands in the waiting line. I can't believe it! I grab a chair and listen to them tell me, one by one, about their personal snow interactions.

I listen to stories from a child who had never seen snow before. "I randed outside to see what it was and forgoted my tennies, and oh my feet got cold, and wetted." Jenny comes without the look of excitement that all the others have. Her head hangs low; her feet drag across the carpet. She says, "I don't have boots at my house. Mom said I had to have boots to go out and play in the snow, so I can't go." My heart falls to the floor with hers. I promise her boots, and I send my assistant out to my car to fetch a pair of my son's boots he left there. He needs new ones anyway.

Sammy politely but firmly declares that she does not like snow and wants no part in it. I reassure her that there are still places in our play area that are sheltered and have received no snow.

There are plans for snowmen and questions about weather. When the children are through talking and I am done listening, we go outside.

Be Someone Children Really Trust

These children demonstrated amazing patience. They knew that if they waited and held the hand of the child in front of them, they would get their turn to speak and have my full, undivided attention. They could trust me to listen with full eye contact, to avoid rushing them or allowing anyone else to interrupt their turn. They were so confident in these facts that some of them waited twenty minutes to have their opportunity to share what was burning to be spoken.

Their confidence had been built over time and with practice. They had tried the Hand-Holding Wait Line before, and it had worked for them. In times past, these very children had stood and waited for their turn. They had experienced my respect as they had their opportunity to share whatever was on their minds. I had listened, fully attentive and sincerely interested. Our relationship was strong. They trusted me, and I did not let them down.

It is a risk to extend trust to another person, and to a three-year-old who has not been shown respect by adults before, it can be very risky indeed. One of the first times I implemented the Hand-Holding Wait Line, Ethan demonstrated his distrust of the whole process. I was helping another child with the spelling of his eight-letter name, and Ethan needed my attention right then. Something about Ethan's truck was extremely important. He ran up and began babbling like a brook. I gently held out my hand to gesture that he could have a turn in a moment, but he refused and began to rush his words louder and faster.

"Ethan, I want to hear all you have to say as soon as I am done with Jonathan. Please hold my hand, and you will be next." It was my well-practiced statement, and it usually worked. Reluctantly, Ethan took my hand. He jiggled from foot to foot and, with his knees' help, managed to jiggle up and down at the same time. My right arm worked as a shock absorber that kept my body from joining in the Jell-O dance. He mumbled quietly as every ounce of his being was rejecting the thought of waiting.

Jonathan was writing his first *a* when Ethan interrupted. "But Miss Cindylee . . ." Again I explained to Ethan that it was rude to interrupt Jonathan, and I assured him that it would only be a moment more and then I would help him with what he needed. The Jell-O dance continued until Jonathan was writing the *h*. At that point, Ethan began to tell Jonathan to hurry up. I reminded Ethan to be patient and encouraged Jonathan to take his time. Now I thought that the dancing Jell-O was going to bounce out of the room. My arm was beginning to tingle.

Jonathan finished his *n* and thanked me for my help. Ethan hurried me to the scene of his broken truck. We pretended to rush his truck to the Mechanics Emergency Room and reassemble the dislodged tire with a screwdriver. While using the screwdriver as a tire iron, I told Ethan that I would always help him, but he needed to remember to wait his turn and to be patient.

I wish I could tell you that from then on Ethan was a model of patience, but that would be far from the truth. In fact, I am not sure the Jell-O jiggle dance ever slowed down. But he did take my hand and trust that I would help him as soon as I could. Patience will probably never be perfect in Ethan, but his trust in me surpassed his inability to be patient. While he could not be patient on his own, his trust in our relationship and my promise to be there for him enabled him to overcome his weakness—to hold hands, jiggle, and wait.

Respectful communication has many aspects. When children trust your words, they know that what you say is what you mean. Children build trust in your words over time. A child knows when you mean what you say. This often has been made evident to me when a parent is leaving with a child. The parent tells the child that she is going to leave, and then she starts a conversation with a teacher or another parent, so the child keeps playing. Then the parent says it again, telling the child to get a coat on or come over to the door, but the parent continues to talk. The child knows that the parent doesn't really mean what she says, so the child continues to play. This may happen a few more times until the parent is irate at the child for not being ready when she finally decides to leave. Looking at a child's reaction to what the adult is saying offers a clue to whether or not the adult means what she says.

Classroom chaos is what you will see if children do not believe what a teacher says. If the teacher has spoken and not followed up on those words, the children will not follow basic instructions. They simply don't believe the teacher really means it. On the flip side, when a teacher follows through with his words, the classroom runs smoothly. Children will even wait their turn to speak.

The adult-child communication should be used primarily for exchanging information and for social contexts. Telling a child that there are more than three thousand different types of butterflies in North America is an exchange of information. When you ask a child how a new pet is doing, you are having a social conversation. Giving instructions should be the smallest portion of the conversations in a classroom. These include statements about it being time to clean up or about washing hands. Instructions about behavior are necessary, but they have the least impact on a child's life.

I once met a professor who ran a classroom without giving any instructions at all. He would make "I" statements, such as: "I want to go outside now. So I am going to pick up these items so we can all go out." Amazingly, the children would follow his actions. They wanted to go out as well, so they helped to clean up. This strategy works really well, especially if you have been playing with the children. They will follow your lead. He would then say, "I want my other friends to go too, so I will see if they need my help." Then he and the group he was playing with would offer to help others to clean up so they could all go out. This approach builds teamwork and strong relationships, but on a deeper level it teaches the children how to think. His statements weren't used just to manipulate behavior. They were models of a type of thinking in his classroom. Children began to make their own "I" statements, proving that he had influenced their thinking processes.

The more you can encourage positive action without giving instructions, the better. It is pretty extreme to say you should never give instructions, but it is best to give as few as possible. Asking questions is a great way to avoid giving instructions. If children come out of the bathroom and are about to go play without washing their hands, ask them what they should do next. It jolts their memory a bit, and they usually know. When you ask children a question, they are doing what they want rather than what someone tells them to do. This makes their behavior their choice and can eliminate an argument from an oppositional or strong-willed child. Save your words for the good stuff, like telling children that there are over two thousand different species of mosquitoes in the whole world and fifty of them live in Minnesota.

Reflection

What an honor it is to have the trust of a child. When I looked down at all eight children standing in that line, I felt like a proud mama duck. Standing there was their way of saying, "I believe you." I had always known the power of a teacher's words, but this was the ultimate testimony. These children knew beyond a shadow of a doubt that I would listen to them when it was their turn. They knew that it was worth the wait. If at any time I had said something and not followed through, their trust would have gone out the window. How powerful truth can be, and how quickly a voided word can devastate.

I have a pet peeve. It happens in the grocery store—or anywhere when a parent is leaving and a child is dragging her feet. The parent says something like, "Hurry up, or I will leave you here." That just gets my goat. There are only two possible truths here. Either the parent is lying to the child, or the parent really would abandon a child. Once I looked down at a child stalling at the end of a grocery aisle and said, "It's okay. If she leaves you, you can come home with me." The parent's eyes grew huge. She picked up her child and almost ran for the door. I don't suggest this; after further thought, I wondered if she would call the police! Even though she was the one threatening to abandon her child, I would have been the one in trouble.

The number one clue that you haven't meant what you said is how well children follow your instructions. This is a telltale sign of whether you have followed through on your words. Children will tell you whether they trust you by how they respond. They will teach you whether your words have power by how they take action or by their lack of action. So take a hard look at how the children respond when you make a request. Is there action or inaction? If you find that the children do not act, do not despair—repair! It's as simple as meaning what you say, saying what you mean, and proving it with your own actions. And if you earn their trust, guard it wisely.

Suggested Reading

Croft, Cindy. 2007. *The six keys: Strategies for promoting children's mental health.* Eden Prairie, MN: Sparrow Media Group.

Howes, Carollee, and Sharon Richie. 2002. *A matter of trust: Connecting teachers and learners in the early childhood classroom.* Foreword by Barbara T. Bowman. New York: Teachers College Press.

4

Mud Day

Today is one of my favorite days of the whole school year. It is Mud Day. For the past week we have been studying soil. Each child brought in a baggy of soil from his or her yard. We looked at all the different colors, talked about what makes up dirt, and viewed the contents under a microscope. We explored different uses for soil in making pottery and farming. We pulled up plants and looked at their roots and how they attached to the soil, and we took a trip to a farm, where we helped a farmer plant his crops. Now it is Friday, and Friday is Mud Day!

We underwent many preparations for Mud Day. We obtained written permission forms from parents, which included instructions about bringing clothes that would never wash clean again. I coordinated with other classes so we would not interrupt their outdoor play events. I gathered hoses and collected old towels. Many parents plan to come during the allotted times to take photos, and a few parents are going to provide an ice cream treat to cool off after Mud Day. The director bought swimming pools, a variety of shovels and pails, and a truckload of unfertilized dirt. We are prepared to add water and make mud for gooshing and squishing and smushing and slushing. We even have a plan for disposing of the gushy mess after Mud Day is over.

There is a tangible buzz when you enter the classroom this morning. Some of the children even arrive dressed in their mud clothes, with clean clothes to put on after hosing off. This is almost bigger than trick or treating! Mud Day is a celebration at the end of the summer. This is our last hurrah before the children go off to kindergarten. We have spent a year together, growing, relating, and learning. I know the children well, and we share a connection that will be celebrated in one last blast of pure fun. I cannot wait!

Then my director walks in. She looks like a sponge that is about to soak up all the excitement, only to dispose of it down the kitchen sink. I know that look; it is a look of "someone called in sick and we have to rearrange children or staff to make the day flow." If she adds children, we may be able to scramble and get permission forms and spare clothes. But if she takes children out so that my assistant can be used somewhere else . . . The thought is unthinkable. We are a small center, and in order to maintain proper adult-to-child ratios we occasionally have to move children around to make it all work. This isn't the best practice for children or staff, but we do what we have to do. A center in a town as small as this struggles to survive.

She starts to speak: "Michelle called in sick; her son has a fever of . . ." Then her voice fades out as my emotions wash over my ears, rendering them useless. There is no sense in arguing the point; I know that she has already done all she could to avoid this action. We combine classrooms, and the day becomes a rush of trying to get permission forms faxed, spare clothes rounded up, and younger children informed. We spend a lot of time making sure the younger children added in will not mishandle the mud, as the children in my class have already been well-versed in mud protocol. The day does not go as smoothly as I planned; I don't get the special time that I hoped for. I don't get those super fun, personal moments with my group. I leave the center at the end of the day feeling disappointed and defeated.

Be Flexible

At the time of the Mud Day I described, I hadn't learned how to success-fully face detours. It pains me now to think how I let my disappointment ruin the moments that could have been. I could have made that detour an exciting event. There were more of us to enjoy the hard work, and more children had the opportunity to learn something new, but I al-lowed my personal feelings to interrupt and limit learning outcomes. My unmet expectations limited my view of possibilities.

Thankfully, since that time, I have changed my outlook. I discovered a new way of thinking on a typical detour route. You see, I live in the land of road construction. Minnesota winters destroy our roads, and many have to be repaired every year. Traffic is rerouted through painstakingly slow alternatives. The first year I lived here, I was late to a job interview and lost a very important opportunity because of road construction. I began to despise detours and rerouting. Such changes would make my blood boil and my stress level rise to its maximum. Detours took me out of my way and destroyed my plans and daily schedules. I had plans! I had schedules! These are too important to be disrupted.

Then one day I had a different type of detour. The route took me through the streets of a small suburb. There were quaint little shops and cute delis with seating at outdoor tables. I was at a dead stand-still for more than twenty minutes as workers cleared an accident a few blocks ahead. The car that was parked on the street just to my right decided it was time to get into our waiting line. As it came in, I moved out. I was already thirty minutes late, and I highly doubted that I would get in to see the doctor I was headed for. So my hunger kicked in, and I pulled over.

I ate at a corner deli that served sandwiches on homemade bread with soup that tasted like Grandma's. Then I walked in and out of art-ists' shops. My favorite was a ceramic store called Doin' the Dishes. It's a place you go to paint ceramics. They provide you with the paint and fire the pieces for you so that you can return in a few days to pick up your artwork. I did not have time that day, but I have visited several times since. The spring sun was shining warmly on me and lightening the weight on my shoulders. The air was fresh, filtering the winter must from my lungs, making it easier to breathe again.

It was a new love affair. This affair began in disgust and developed into a new passion. Detours became an opportunity for me to discover something new, to encounter some hidden treasure off the beaten path, and to venture in new directions. Now I see detours as opportunities to open my mind and look beyond the normal, beyond the expected. They still disrupt my schedule, so I have learned to adjust, but the adjustments are less painful, and the cost is worth the outcome.

Now I also choose to see the detours in my daily classroom routines and schedules as blessings. I take the time to see what a child is really pointing at, to discover what the real need is. What beauty or area of interest is the child trying to detour me toward? I have discovered many things during these classroom detours. I have discovered a child's determination to learn to tie his shoes. I have seen a child's embarrassment over not making it to the restroom on time and helped her rise above the embarrassment to take a new look at the situation. I have been able to support children in solving their own problems, taking initiative, building friendships. I have taken detours with children to areas I would have missed otherwise, areas of growth, change, and development. All these things are detours in our regularly scheduled events, detours of beauty that now I would not miss for the world. I wish I could relive Mud Day. It would have ended differently.

Having a schedule and ideas in place for a class is important. These visions and goals lead to classroom plans, and plans provide purposeful teaching. Plans can be carried out during the day with different types of teaching—such as theme-based or emergent, to list two common strategies. Regardless of what style you choose, if you want to introduce new ideas, increase knowledge, challenge the learner, and be effective, you must have goals that are represented in some form of a basic plan.

Within the plan for the day there are routines. The most common routine is going outside. Almost every teacher I have met has a routine based on steps she follows to transition children from indoor to outdoor experiences. There is a routine for using the restroom. There is a routine for donning weather-appropriate clothing. There is a routine for waiting for the others to finish their tasks and a routine for exiting the building. Then there is the common result—outside, or at least you hope so.

I moved to Minnesota several years ago, and my biggest shock was taking twenty children out to play in the snow. Each child needed to put on snow pants, boots, mittens or gloves, a scarf, a hat, and a coat that had to be zipped—all of this times twenty, plus two teachers. It took me a month to establish smooth routines. Then it never failed; as soon as all were zipped up, someone needed to use the restroom. It didn't matter that they had all just gone fifteen minutes before; someone needed to go again. So off with the gloves, off with the coat to undo the snow pants to get to the inside pants . . . You get the picture. I am not sure why it all bothered me so much, but I found it entirely irritating that as soon as we were ready to go out, someone had to use the bathroom.

The number one and most common frustration teachers face is the breaking of routines and processes. We expect that all the children will follow the routine. A child who steps outside it disrupts the process and causes complications. Things do not go as we expect, and now we need to take time to get the child back into the flow. This causes delays and frustration. Our expectations for the day have been broken, and it might lead to a domino effect that can throw the morning off—or even make the whole day feel out of whack.

Broken or unmet expectations are difficult to handle, and as professionals we have to choose how we are going to respond to them. We can see them as road blocks in our day, disrupting and maybe even destroying our plans. That's when we begin to despise these detours. That's also when the negativity will show in our tone of voice as we try to hurry up the detoured child. If you choose to go down that road, your level of effectiveness will be worn away.

There is another response to detours. We need to remember this option: detours can take us to places of beauty.

Reflection

How do you view interruptions in your day? Are they obstacles that distract and destroy your flow, or are they new adventures with great plot lines? For a person who enjoys change, detours can be a pleasant change of pace. For the person who prefers routine, detours can be a challenge to peace of mind. Neither view is right or wrong, but how you react can be enabling or disabling. Chances are that if you do not enjoy change or impulsivity, you will never truly relish detours in your day. But you do not have to allow them to limit you.

Things to Keep in Mind about Detours

1. Evaluate the disruptions of your day. There might be a few each day, but if there are more disruptions than routines, you may have a deeper problem. Each day should be a smooth road with a few detours—not a road of chaos with a few smooth spots.
2. Start each morning with the awareness that everything may not go perfectly, but vow to find the beauty in the detours.
3. Verbalize the detours in your day. Example: "We didn't plan on it raining today, but since it is, we can use our rainy day plan." It is good for children to hear how you handle detours. You might even state that you are disappointed that it is raining, but you don't want to let it ruin the fun. Verbalizing your determination to overcome a detour will also help you develop a good attitude yourself.

Me, Biased? No Way!

Have you ever not liked a child? I'm not just talking about the child's behavior, but the actual child. Maybe her personality rubs you the wrong way, or his mannerisms just irk you. Teachers are individuals too; we have preferences and personalities. It takes all kinds of people to make the world go 'round, and I am sure that the people whom I don't enjoy being around have their perfect place in this world. But it is not near me! Let me introduce you to one of them—Darrin—and yes, his name has been changed.

It is lunchtime. Our kitchen was designed to be extra big. We have a table that can easily sit ten adults, two high chairs, several countertops, and all the regular stuff that fits into a kitchen, with a pantry off to the side. I enjoy sitting with all the children around our kitchen table, laughing and eating lunch. Today is chicken-and-rice casserole day. The plates are set, the milk is cold, and the hungry tummies are finishing putting away their toys so they can all get full. I am helping our newest member, Darrin, find where to put the puzzle back on the shelf. He gently puts the last piece of wooden apple into its matching cutout spot on the puzzle board. Then, as if in slow motion, he stands and stares, waits, and then sluggishly puts one hand on one side of the puzzle, and the other hand on the other side. As if he has to think about what to do, he lifts it up. Then, leisurely, he takes the five steps to the shelf and carefully places the puzzle in its spot. I walk out of the play room toward the kitchen; when I turn to talk to him, he isn't there. I go back to see that he has only progressed about four steps. Each leg seems to move as if it were in molasses.

"We are having lunch now in the kitchen. Are you hungry?" I am secretly trying to hurry him up. His eyes meet mine as he walks toward me. His head nods, but his feet don't seem to move any faster.

"I'll meet you in the kitchen." I walk back to the kitchen, help the youngest two wash their hands, and buckle the youngest of those into a high chair. Everyone is seated when Darrin finally makes it into the room. His eyes are bright, and his smile is delightful, but my patience is wearing thin—and I consider myself to have a great deal to wear away at. My hair is standing up on the back of my neck. My respirations per minute have just doubled.

"Let's go in to wash your hands, Darrin. Everyone is waiting to begin eating." (Everyone except for our high chair occupant.) I finally decide to give him a little help with speed before his waiting classmates begin to complain. I pick him up and boost him to the top of the stool to wash his hands. We sing the "Washy Washy" song, and I whisk him into his chair.

My heart is aching. How could I not like a child? I have always viewed each child as special and lovable. In fact, until this very moment, I haven't met a child I did not like. There must be a developmental issue. That would make sense. Then I could at least understand why he moves so slowly. In order to relieve my guilt, I speak with a developmental and occupational therapist, who agrees to come and meet Darrin. She isn't doing a formal assessment. She is just going to let me know if she thinks we should pursue that avenue.

My heart aches again when she informs me that she sees no reason for concern. I am totally irritated by this child. I am terrible. I feel horrible. This child needs nurturing, acceptance, and loving care, and I have a hard time even watching him. How pathetic I am!

Build a Relationship with Every Child

Darrin was two when we first met. I was operating a family child care. On his first day in our home, I knew I had issues. *He* was fine; this was definitely my problem. I am a fast-paced person. I get great satisfaction from filling my days with incredible quantities of things to accomplish, and I hold myself to them. Some say I am a workaholic; I say I just have a high level of productivity. Darrin, however, moved very slowly. I mean *very slowly*. Like a sloth, okay? He moved like a sloth! Maybe it was not that bad, but on some days it seemed like it. He walked slowly, and we always had to wait for him. He moved slowly going from room to room; he moved slowly when we played games. When we sang, he was always a word or two behind. He was intelligent and followed instructions well. His communication was great. He showed no signs of delay. He just liked to take his time.

I confided in a friend who was also a provider. She gave me great advice. She said, "Spend more time with him." That seemed odd. I was already having problems with the time we *did* spend together, and she wanted me to spend more time with him? But the goal was to develop a relationship with him. I needed to get to know him better, to appreciate his talents, preferences, and abilities.

So I began to play with Darrin and spend more time with him. At first it was difficult, but I needed to look past the personality trait and see the child. He had a unique ability to see details that all the rest of us rush by. Here's how I first found that out.

We were outside. Darrin was sitting in the grass near the hedge. I was playing ball with Jason and Denise. Children were riding bikes on the path and painting with water on the fence. It was a perfect spring day. Everything was finally green and colorful. The smells of the neighbor's freshly cut grass lingered, making my grass jealous. The elm trees shaded us from the midday sun, and the birds sang overhead. Darrin was still staring at the hedge. I went to see what was up.

"Hey, Darrin, what's up?"

"Nothing," he replied.

"Are you okay?"

"Yep."

"Do you need my help?"

"Nope, I'm good."

I invited him to join our ball game or one of the other activities, but he insisted that he was fine. Several minutes later Darrin was still staring at the bush. I meandered over and sat beside him.

"Hey, Darrin, what's up?"

"Nothing."

I had been here before, so I tried a different road. I began to stare at the bush, at the spot he was watching. On a leaf about a foot into the bush was a tiny baby caterpillar. Then I widened my gaze, and there were a few more and a few more. At least twenty leaves were occupied by tiny baby caterpillars. They couldn't have been more than a half-inch long. They were half-inching along, and they were beginning to eat the leaves.

Darrin pointed to one of the leaves and said, "This one just came out. I think he's the last one." Darrin had been sitting there watching caterpillars hatch! I slowly encouraged the other kids to come and watch this spectacular event of nature. This led to weeks of learning. We followed many of the caterpillars through the life cycle, until they became butterflies. Then they flew away. That day Darrin walked up to me and plainly, slowly said, "They are all gone now."

I began to appreciate Darrin's incredible eye. He shared dazzling views of the world. We used magnifying glasses to look at tiny rainbows that he found in the morning dew. We used stethoscopes to hear the wind that the heater made in the floor. We spun the wheel of an upside-down tricycle and listened to the whistling tunes that different sticks made as they slid on the tire. Not only did I appreciate Darrin, but I actually enjoyed him. I still got irritated while waiting a long time for him to act, but the annoyance lessened over time, stamped out by the admiration of his special gift to see the smallest of details and delights.

We all know that every child is as different as his fingerprint, no two alike. Eventually we are bound to find one we don't enjoy. There are children who seem mean and children who come from home not smelling so great. Some children are angry because of their personal circumstances. Some children just irritate us. Being nonjudgmental, accepting, and caring will be difficult at times. The way to get past your inhibitions as a teacher is to see the positive, even if you have to hunt for it.

With Darrin, the trick was to see his special talents and abilities. With another child, you may need to find a way to help him heal, or you might have to teach her parents proper hygiene. We have to look beyond the surface, beyond the obvious, and find the child who lies beneath.

Reflection

Darrin's story was a tough one. I questioned my choice of occupation, my motives, my professionalism, my calling. I questioned everything about myself. It was a very sobering time in my life and my career. I had forgotten that I come with my own personality, my own preferences, and my own bias—I responded as if being a teacher somehow put all those things aside. Over time, I learned that with professionalism I can limit the effect that my personal opinions have on my day-to-day work with kids, but I need to be always aware and alert for when they try to sneak back in. We are emotionally vested in our work. If we weren't, we wouldn't be any good at it.

"Bias" is a small word with a big meaning. There are many studies on gender and racial biases, and personal preferences can cause bias as well. It is easy to enjoy the cute or pretty kids, but those who aren't so pretty can be a little tougher to enjoy. It takes awareness of your own feelings about different situations to ward off bias. Don't be surprised when it hits you. Our upbringing and experiences affect our biases. We can say we are antibias, but we never know what might open our eyes to a different story.

Are you conscious of how you feel toward different children or why you feel that way? Take stock of your responses to their behavior. How do you feel about the children who make your job a bit more challenging? These are difficult questions; don't be afraid of the answers.

Suggested Reading

Jacobson, Tamar. 2003. *Confronting our discomfort: Clearing the way for anti-bias in early childhood.* Portsmouth, NH: Heinemann.

6

Vincent's Story

There is a child I did not enjoy knowing. My aversion to this child was his behavior—or should I say his learned behavior. Vincent was aggressive; I would even call him violent. When a child had a toy he wanted, Vince would walk up and push the child and grab the toy. If a child was in line ahead of him, he would walk to the front and shove his way in without regard for the damage it might cause someone else. On this day, Vince's behavior reached a particularly difficult point.

We are waiting for the rest of the class to put on their coats to go outside. Vince gets ready, walks straight to the front, and uses two hands to shove the child who is unfortunate enough to be first in line. He pushes so hard that the front child is shoved back on top of the other three behind him. They are left in a pile of hurt bodies. Vince turns around and stands where the line begins.

When we talk with Vince about his actions, he says nothing. When we move him out of line to wait for the rest of the class to go first, he says nothing. Finally, I ask him why he hurts people. His reply appalls me. I am shocked—not at him, but at his parents.

He says, "My dad is the gang leader, and he teaches me to do it. I am to take whatever I want, and when I tell him I hurt people, he laughs and gives me hugs." I feel physically sick. And this situation leads to my first time dealing with Child Protective Service.

Be Prepared to Help Abused Children

Child abuse and early childhood education are in direct opposition of one another. Everything that we stand for, that we strive for, that we promote, child abuse undoes. It is our adversary, our opposition, our number one enemy. It is the "big ugly" that you can find yourself facing. You need to arm yourself with proper tools to face this opponent. You will need shields of love and compassion, nerves of steel, an iron resolve, and swift feet to act. Your words and questions need to be wise. Saying the wrong thing can add to the damage, and asking the wrong questions can abort a court's ability to act.

It is not our job to investigate. It is our job to report what we know. We do not decide whether to pursue legal action against the alleged abuser. We just report to the state's Child Protective Service (CPS); that agency's representatives are trained to know when to act and when not to act. We must be accurate, detailed, and cautious not to overdramatize or let our judgment get in the way of facts.

Confidentiality is paramount when you suspect abuse or neglect. Some agencies say you shouldn't even speak with the center director or your supervisor, but should just call a protective agency directly. You should know your state's and employer's policies regarding confidentiality. If you work in this business, it is not a matter of whether you will encounter possible abuse, but when.

Reflection

The following excerpt from *Caregivers of Young Children: Preventing and Responding to Child Maltreatment* (U.S. Department of Health and Human Services 1992) provides information I want you to know, that children need you to know. Prepare yourself before you need to be prepared. Believe me: your heart will race, you will question what your ears tell you, and you will feel emotions you never thought possible. Rage was the emotion I felt and had no prior experience with, and then I mixed in doses of adrenalin and poured it all over a broken heart.

> When children's verbal skills are advanced enough for them to participate in conversations, they may be able to answer questions about their injuries or other signs of maltreatment. The caregiver should keep in mind that the child may be hurt, in pain, fearful, or apprehensive. Every effort must be made to keep the child as comfortable as possible during the discussion.
>
> The primary purpose for the discussion is to gather enough information from the child to make an informed report to the CPS agency. Once the essential information has been gathered, the caregiver should conclude the conversation. *When the early childhood education professional is talking with the child, he/she is not conducting an interrogation and is not trying to prove that abuse or neglect has occurred.*
>
> The person who talks with the child should be someone the child trusts and respects, such as a caregiver, family child care provider, or teacher. The conversation should be conducted in a quiet, private, nonthreatening place that is familiar to the child. In nice weather, a pleasant spot outdoors might be appropriate.
>
> For example, a teacher might see the child alone in the book corner reading a book. She could sit with the child, strike up a conversation, and try, in the course of the conversation, to steer

the discussion toward his/her injuries. She might say, "I noticed that new bruise on your arm this morning. It must have hurt when you got it. Would you like to talk about it?" The teacher should then wait to see if the child wants to talk about the bruise or change the subject to something else. If the child changes the subject, the teacher should go along with the change in conversation and not push the child to talk about the injury.

When children are willing to discuss their injuries, they should be reassured that they have done nothing wrong. Maltreated children often feel, or are told, that they are to blame for their own abuse or neglect and for bringing trouble to the family. Therefore, it is important to reassure children that they are not at fault. The caregiving professional talking with the child must be very careful not to show any verbal or nonverbal signs of shock or anger when the child is talking about what happened to cause the injury.

It is important for caregivers of young children to use terms and language the child can understand. If a child uses a term that is not familiar (such as a word for a body part), the caregiving professional may ask for clarification or ask the child to point to the body part he/she means. Caregivers of young children should not make fun of or correct the child's words; it is better to use the same words to put the child at ease and to avoid confusion. If the child is showing sexual knowledge that is inappropriate for that age group, the caregiver could ask in a quiet, low-key tone, "Where did you learn about . . . ?"

Children should not be pressed for answers or details that they may be unable or unwilling to give. For example, it would be inappropriate to ask, "Did you get that bruise when someone hit you?" If the child changes what he/she has already said, the caregiver should just listen and note the change. The caregiving professional should not ask "why" questions. *Caregivers of young children can actually do the child more harm by probing for answers or supplying the child with terms or information.* Several major child sexual abuse cases have been dismissed in court because it was felt that the initial interviewers biased the children.

If children want to show their injuries, the caregiver should allow them to do so. But if a child is unwilling to show an injury, the caregiver should not insist, and, of course, no child should be pressured to remove clothing.

Caregivers must be sensitive to the safety of the child following the disclosure; the child might be subject to further abuse if he/she goes home and mentions talking with someone at the program. If a caregiver of young children feels that the child is in danger, CPS should be contacted immediately. Support from CPS may provide protection for the child. A CPS caseworker may need to interview the child at the program. If so, the program should provide a private place for the interview, and a caregiver, teacher, or provider whom the child trusts should be present throughout the interview. If it is necessary for the CPS caseworker to remove the child from the program for a medical examination, caregivers should request a written release from the CPS caseworker.

PART TWO

Help Me Feel Special

7

Brave Art Princess

Tears erupt from the art table. On my way across the room, I can see Ella's sad face. "Ella, why are you sad?" I kneel beside her.

"Tana says my horse is wrong." I look at her crayon drawing. It is a purple, four-legged animal with long legs and a mane of pink. The horse has black dots for eyes and a smile. The bottom of the page has flowers of red and yellow with a green base.

"It's purple. She says it's wrong because horses are supposed to be brown." Ella feels humiliated and hurt by her friend's words. Tana continues to color in the blue sky that surrounds her "correct" brown horse. She sits tall, knowing that she is right; horses in her world are all brown.

"Ella, this is art. There are never any wrongs in art." I look her squarely in the eyes. "You are a brave person to draw a purple horse. Most people do draw their horses colors that we already see on horses, but you, you drew your horse in a way I have never seen before. You have allowed me to see something new and different. That is really hard to do. It took a lot of guts. You are my Art Hero; you are a brave, beautiful Art Princess."

I wish I could show you the picture she draws next. It is a purple princess—a brave, strong, purple Art Princess. And Tana? She draws a pink horse.

Let Children Be Unique

It was quite the revelation, that moment with Ella. There aren't any wrongs in art. Whatever the artist does is right. I wonder where this stuff comes from sometimes. I knew Ella was a "unique"; she saw the world differently than her classmates. I have been honored to meet a few unique people in my lifetime. They see things in a way I never thought of before. They have a perspective that is uncommon yet uncovers truth.

I once gave a standardized test to a five-year-old, and one of the tasks was to draw a line under the drawing of a balloon. Most five-year-olds drew the line like a string, a sight they are most familiar with. On a very rare occasion a child would underline the balloon, which was the correct response according to the manual. This child turned the paper over and drew a line on the page so that when he turned it back over the line was literally *under* the balloon. He had an uncommon perspective that uncovered an unexpected truth. His solution was more "right" than any other had been.

Ella was truly unique. She had a unique relationship with music. She could feel the flow of music and express it with her body in a totally pure form. She hadn't watched hours of MTV to copy the movements. I have seen small children copying movement that is hardly appropriate for grown adults, let alone young children. (Whoops, my age is showing!) Anyway, the point is that Ella was creating her own movements. It was quite beautiful to watch. There were times when her arms gracefully floated like a butterfly. At other times, when the music would speed up, she seemed to imitate a fat bumblebee. But the movement was always just Ella—pure, uninhibited, and enchanting.

What would happen if her parents put her in dance class? I was worried that it would destroy the natural beauty of her dance. When the day came that they told me she was beginning dance classes, I smiled on the outside, but I cringed inside. Dance class could hinder or even eliminate her self-expression. They would show her the "right" way to do it; all other ways would become wrong. Her way would become wrong. She would be wrong. The very essence that filled her little soul would be labeled as wrong.

The morning after her first dance class, Ella showed me some of the steps that they had introduced in the class. She gave a brief recital before she broke out in butterfly-like fluid movement. Maybe there was hope.

Two days later, it was dance night. Mom brought Ella's required dance class attire to school and asked me to have Ella in it at four forty-five PM. Class started at five, and Mom was already stressed about getting there on time. Tardiness was not tolerated. But at four thirty, when I figured we had ample time, Ella said no. She said it simply at first and then stated it rather loudly, "NO." She was resisting? She resisted me until four forty-five; then she resisted her mom. Mom gave in, allowing Ella to skip the tights and just wear the leotard. I don't recall any other time when Mom ever gave in—ever.

The next morning Mom told us her story of humiliation. Ella had totally, purposefully ignored the teacher while doing her own thing. The other children watched Ella and decided what she was doing was more fun. They joined her. Oh my goodness, Mom was a mess. The class had totally fallen apart, the other moms were irate, and the instructor said that if Ella couldn't follow instructions, she couldn't be in the class. Mom's first question to me was whether Ella followed instructions in my class. Of course Ella did, and I reassured her mom of the fact.

I wondered if Ella needed to get a solid grip on her own self-expression before being willing to learn it any other way. Maybe her talent was so unique that she recognized she would lose what was deep in her if it got replaced with formal training at such a young age. I thought Ella was a "unique" and more beautiful than any taught dancer anyway.

Being unique at the age of four can be difficult. We teach children how to do things all day long. We teach them how to tie their shoes, how to brush their teeth, and how not to show us their teeth at the lunch table. They learn at a young age that there is a right way and a wrong way to do things. This can inhibit their freedom to be unique. If we teach them there is only one way to dance or a right way to color a horse, we are forcing our limitations on another human being. Yes, there are some rules to painting. For example, if you leave paint in the paintbrush, it won't be much good the next time. Another one of my favorite limits is that if you paint on the wall, you will ruin your painting when you wash it off. But feel free to put anything on paper that you would like. You can ask for a bigger piece of paper—even wall-sized—and I will see what I can do. But on the wall, art doesn't work so well. There are times when we need to follow the rules. Rules are generally for safety and order. For example, I wouldn't want any driver deciding to be unique on a road near me. Rules give us the guidelines to exist positively in our community.

Some classroom rules, however, may just be for our convenience and may not be necessary. One rule I find myself constantly challenging is what I call the "don't bring it over here" rule. This rule states that the blocks stay in the block area, and the books stay in the book area. This rule does bring order to the room. But it limits creativity. What harm does it do to bring blocks into the kitchen to make chicken noodle soup? Yes, the children will scatter things everywhere. And yes, you will spend more time cleaning up. But if you teach children responsibility, including cleaning up their own messes, they will gain so much. The freedom of the imagination, within safe guidelines, needs to be honored.

We need to hunt for opportunities to allow children to freely express their individuality and uniqueness. Otherwise, twenty years from now, there will be no art or beautiful dancing, only well-conformed ducks all marching in a row.

I raised a "unique," my middle child, Levi. When he was two years old, we were carrying groceries out to the car when his feet switched directions. "Slide, Mama—I want slide." He was pointing toward a hillside of homes, but for the life of me, I did not see any slide. He insisted and pointed repeatedly. I put the groceries in the car and asked him to show me.

"Right there." He pointed, using large, direct pointing.

"I don't see it, Levi. It looks like you're pointing at the road."

"Uh-uh, slide, Mama, car slide." Sure enough! The road came straight down the middle of the hill, and it sloped just like a straight slide. Of course, we drove down the slide many times with long cries of "Wheee!" He grew up and continues to bring a unique point of view to the world.

After the drawing of the Brave Art Princess, I began to make all the art materials available to the children in my class. I wanted them to be free to express themselves in any way they chose with as many options as I could possibly provide. All art was heralded as being right. I gave them instructions as to how to take care of the materials, but I let them have free rein. They could use whatever they wanted to as long as it was done respectfully. This had incredible results. The children created masterpieces that I never would have thought they were capable of. Some were expressions of pure color; some resembled items in real life. Some children spent hours at the art table, others only moments. It took a few months of developing skills and practice, but then they began to be true expressive artists.

We even prepared an art show. One of the students decided he wanted to make one really perfect piece. So we created the following instructions for making a masterpiece.

1. Draw many sketches of possible ideas. (He drew ten different ideas.)
2. From the sketches pick one to develop.
3. Decide what medium or media you will use.

4. Make the first attempt.

5. Analyze what you like and what you want to change, and do it again.

6. Analyze again and make the final piece.

We took photos of him working, saved all the preliminary work, and then included it in the art show. We started at the beginning of the room and displayed his work in the order in which it was developed. When the parents came, he stood with pride and explained the procedure for creating a masterpiece to anyone who would listen—and even to some who wouldn't.

We all must abide by certain social rules. We choose to abide by certain moral codes. But uniqueness and individuality, within social and moral guidelines, ought to exist freely.

As adults we are often limited by peer pressure or fear of rejection. I couldn't get up and dance the way Ella did, even if my moves were as beautiful. Dancing like that would be different and odd. As an adult I am limited by social expectations and find it difficult to freely express my opinions and talents. It is the uniqueness that makes art beautiful. It is the uniqueness that makes dance beautiful. In adults it is the fear of uniqueness that limits our expressions. Those who overcome the fear, or who were never given it as a child, often create great things for the rest of us to enjoy.

Reflection

In the story of the Art Princess, a great tragedy occurred. Ella was demeaned for expressing her true self. She felt not only that her art was wrong, but that *she* was wrong. If she were expressing herself and it was wrong, then she could only come to the conclusion that her very being was wrong. The essence of Ella—indeed, her quintessence—was attacked. I became aware that protecting the children in my class also included protecting their personalities. I was their freedom protector, defending their right to be right.

I feel that every person, young and old, can expand my views. They can teach me something, or they can help me to understand something I didn't understand before. They can broaden my perspective.

Generally, as adults, we know all the ways we are supposed to behave. We have mastered the art of blending into society. Children need to learn the social rules that keep us all living in harmony (for the most part). But conforming at the risk of losing individuality is unacceptable. Just as we appreciate cultural differences, we need to appreciate individual differences.

Where are the limitations in your room? Are they limits that need to be in place for safety or learning?

When do we limit children? It is okay to limit how many children wash their hands in a sink at one time. This is a safety issue. But are we limiting freedom of play and expression? Sometimes we limit play based on children's physical abilities, and that is necessary for their safety. But if we are limiting play for our convenience, we can inhibit their growth and education.

Suggested Reading

Althouse, Rosemary, Margaret H. Johnson, and Sharon T. Mitchell. 2003. *The colors of learning: Integrating the visual arts into the early childhood curriculum.* New York: Teachers College Press; Washington, DC: National Association for the Education of Young Children.

Pelo, Ann. 2007. *The language of art: Inquiry-based studio practices in early childhood settings.* Saint Paul: Redleaf Press.

8

Hyper-Organized, Bo-Established Systems

It is Friday morning, and all the little boxes on my "goals for the week" chart are checked off, except for one—Bo's individual goal for the week. There it is, staring me in the face: "Bo will complete one routine task in a new way this week." Bo gets stuck in a routine rut. Everything must go as it has the day before, or he becomes insecure and upset. His reaction is so severe that it impairs his ability to try new things. For him, everything needs to be the same, done the same way as before, or it just isn't right. I must find a way to help Bo appreciate change and new ideas.

The morning proceeds as usual and now is half gone; I still have no success with my Bo goal. Most children are putting away toys and equipment, getting ready for lunch. Bo heads for the blocks as he always does. He likes them to be put on the shelf in a hyper-organized, Bo-established system. This is my opportunity. I jump in to help him. Randomly, carelessly, I put all the blocks on the shelf.

"Teacher Cindawee [I will always remember the way he says my name], that is not how they go."

"It's okay, Bo. What if we try it my way today?"

"No, it doesn't work like that. They go all lineded up," Bo emphatically explains.

"Well, why? I like them like this; it is okay to be different and to do things differently. Today I think we ought to put the blocks away all messed up." I spend the next few minutes in this conversation. I explain that everyone has a unique way of doing things. Sometimes it is different from what we are used to, but it's good to be different and try new things.

Bo reiterates more firmly, "No, the blocks must go on the shelf in the right way!" Bo is getting red. The other kids finish and begin to gather around.

"I think we should put all the big ones on the bottom," Tori offers. So I pull them all onto the floor in a heap and ask her to show me. Bo is beginning to break into a sweat. He practices more patience than most adults, yet as each student takes turns rearranging the blocks, he says that it isn't right. It is lunchtime, so we leave the blocks the way the last child arranges them. Bo walks to the hand-washing area, shoulders slumped, head dropped, feet barely lifted up to move forward drudgingly, painfully slowly.

Have I gone too far? I had been hoping for flexibility, acceptance. What I have is a young boy defeated. Have I pushed too hard? Have I crushed his little heart? Did I check off my list at the expense of a child?

We both are slumping when lunch arrives, tomato soup and grilled cheese sandwiches. The crackers come in individually wrapped packages. Toddler teachers despise anything that comes individually wrapped, but my older preschoolers can pretty much open them by themselves.

Then it happens. Bo looks up and states, "There are twelve ways to open crackers. You can open them with your fingers. You can open them with your teeth. You can open them by yourself, and you can open them with a friend."

The whole class begins to join in, and I grab a pen.

"You can open them up high."

"You can open them down low."

"You can open them fast or slow."

"You can crunch up the crackers first."

"You can crunch them up last."

"You can open them with one hand."

"You can open them with two hands."

"You can use three hands, but four doesn't work so well."

Bo finishes our poem, "There are probably more ways than that, but I can only think of twelve. It is good to try it differently today." Bo smiles, and my shoulders quit slumping.

I check to make sure every child is resting after lunch. As I round the last corner, I pass by the block shelf. I laugh out loud. Sure enough, those blocks are back in the hyper-organized, Bo-established system.

Identify and Honor Each Child's Talents

Every child has a personality, talents, and preferences that are unique. These gifts and talents need to be appreciated and accepted. I imagine today Bo is organizing a huge business deal somewhere. As a child he had a natural gift for organization. His coat was always hung nice and straight. His papers for his parents were lined up neatly. When I needed help picking up or organizing our room, he was the one I went to. But organization at the cost of acceptance and flexibility would have narrowed his vision of possibility, and at three years old he was too young to eliminate possibility from his life.

Some children are born leaders, and some are born artists. I have met three-year-old scientists who notice even the smallest changes in a growing plant. I have enjoyed the music of preschool composers and vocalists. With every child there are different abilities and talents. If you look, you will see their gifts. You can see it in the way they spend hours constructing, organizing, or talking. You can see it in the thinker whose thoughts cannot yet be put into words.

There are children who have a strong sense of empathy, and they go around making sure everyone is okay. Children who are helpers get a great feeling of accomplishment when they help people. Some children live life with great passion. Often they are called Drama Queens or Drama Kings, but they feel things very deeply. Judicial children have a need to have everything be fair. To them, life is black and white, with gray being intolerable. I have already discussed the unique ones, the ones who give us beautiful things.

I met one child who loved to run. He ran just for the sake of running. In fact, if he did not have ample opportunity to run, he would start crying. He didn't really know why. But if I took him outside and let him run in circles for about fifteen minutes, all the tears would be gone, and he could interact and focus again. His need to run was so deep that it affected him emotionally.

Can you imagine a class where every child had the opportunity to do what he was good at? The leaders could lead, and the helpers could help. The tenderhearted could assist those who were hurt, and the runner could lead outdoor time. How happy the children would be, doing what they love, doing what they are good at! I know that when I am doing what I love to do, I feel very complete and satisfied.

We can provide children with opportunities to use their individual talents and abilities. We can teach the leader to lead, provide the artist more media to experiment with, and give the scientist more opportunities to explore. All children need equal access to all these areas, but when we recognize a talent in a child, we should give that child ample opportunity to develop it to the fullest.

Talents are often unrecognized by those who own them. This is because the talent is so natural and such a part of the person that she does not see it as special. She just assumes everyone is like this. I never knew that I had a gift for working with children until someone pointed it out to me.

I had taken my kids to the park. They were between the ages of three and seven years old. They were doing what they loved. Monica was swinging, Jason had a ball, and Levi was running after it. There were probably ten or so other children in the park with us. I don't know where their parents were. It was a safe neighborhood park, and one or two parents were sitting off to the side, but I was the only adult interacting with the kids. Pretty soon, I was the organizer of a kickball game. They played, and I made sure all the rules were intact and all the players were safe and having fun. I cheered when the kicker kicked a good one. I cheered when they made a play, and I encouraged them when they missed it. We played until it was too dark to be safe kicking around a ball anymore. They whined when I said we were through. They begged me to come back the next day.

One of the parents who had been watching on the sidelines came up and simply said, "Did you know that you are great with kids? Not everyone could do what you do." At first, I thought it was an odd thing to say. Surely anyone could referee a kickball game. That wasn't what she was referring to. It was the cheering and encouraging and seeing children and their needs. To top it off, I enjoyed it! I had a talent that I had not recognized. It was so easy for me; I was just being myself. Someone—I don't even know her name—pointed out to me that I had a talent, an ability that not everyone had, and she appreciated it. For me it was a catalyst; it changed the entire course of my life. It was then that I decided to make early childhood education a career.

In our moments, days, and years with young children, it is our responsibility to honor the individuality of everyone we guide and teach. We can help the children and their parents discover each child's talents and abilities. We can give them opportunities to grow in these areas. Many times I have told children that they have great talents, and their reactions have varied. I remember telling one boy that he had a great mind for details. He asked me what that was, and I told him that all the trivia and knowledge that he had in his head was special, that not everyone can remember all that stuff.

He said, "Like when I remember that the adult human head weighs about ten pounds and that a pound cake doesn't really weigh a pound?"

I nodded. "Not all people can remember those details like you can."

He just said, "Huh," and walked off. But when his dad came to pick him up, the boy asked him if he knew how much the adult human head weighed. His dad shook his head, and the child just smiled. "Ten pounds, Dad, ten pounds."

Reflection

Bo's reaction scared me at first. I thought that maybe I had pushed him too hard. We shared a slump. Thankfully, he began to see a new perspective, and I was relieved that I hadn't hurt his emotional well-being and self-esteem. It could have gone that way. I could have made him feel that because he wasn't right about the blocks, he, as a person, wasn't right. The fact that he returned all the blocks back to his preferred positioning made me feel that he was going to be okay.

There are times as a teacher when you wonder if you have done the wrong thing—responded to children in a way that hurt their feelings or misspoken to a parent. In fact, chances are that at some point in your career these things will happen. We are not perfect. We are growing and learning and maturing along with those we spend energy trying to help grow and learn and mature. With Bo I had been successful. But I have many of these stories without the pretty ending. I have, at times, created a mess that I have had to take responsibility for and clean up.

During my college years, too long ago to tell you when, flannelboard stories were thought of as a cutting-edge teaching practice. I, however, am flannelboard impaired. It never makes sense when I try it. This seems silly, I know, but I cannot tell a proper flannelboard story to save my life. I have redemption, though—give me a puppet, and I can teach the world.

What are your talents? Remember, they may not seem special to you because using them seems so easy.

Do you think that children show their lifelong talents when they are this young?

Does it matter? I don't think it can hurt to tell a child that she is good at something, as long as it is true.

How many talents or abilities can you name? I'll get you started:

Tenderhearted	Scientific
Compassionate	Detail-oriented
Artistic	Dramatic
Supportive	Mathematical
Creative	Analytical
Passionate	Athletic
Leader	Empathetic
Helper	Nurturing

Keep adding to this list. The more children you meet, the more your list will grow.

At the beginning of the story about Bo, I mentioned that I have a weekly goal chart. This chart includes a weekly goal I set for each child—something that will help to develop a personal talent area. Some examples would be to teach a leader to have better communication skills or more polite ways to lead, or to give a quieter child the opportunity to express thoughts in a safe environment where he has no fear of being humiliated or ridiculed. I write notes to the parents to let them know what their child's goal is, and when it is reached, I record it for them in a journal. This also helps to build parents' appreciation of their child's gifts.

In appendix B you can find copies of these tools. I use the Individual Goal Chart as my checklist, to make sure I attend to every goal. I also highlight my lesson plan to indicate which activities or time slots I have planned with individual goals in mind. I fill out an Individual Goal

Sheet for parents. You'll see that the bottom third of the sheet is labeled "Notes." Here I write notes about how the activities went. This sheet with the notes goes home to parents with next week's new goal sheet. This helps all of us to see the progress we are making.

Suggested Reading

Burt, Sandra, and Linda Perlis. 2007. *Raising a successful child: Discover and nurture your child's talents*. Berkeley: Ulysses Press.

Leader in Disguise

Abby is a loud, round, red-headed five-year-old. She did not come with a volume adjustment, and asking for "inside voices" just means that more people can hear her. Today, the chairs are lined up in a row, occupied by children bobbing their heads and singing, "The wheels on the bus go 'round and 'round . . ." Abby is driving, of course.

"Stop!" she says. It is amazing how her one spoken word overpowers the voices of ten others.

"You get off here," are her orders as she points to one of the riders.

"I don't want to get off," he pleads.

"You get off here," she repeats and waits. He meanders off the bus, feeling sad and excluded. His three buddies join him.

"You don't get off here," the driver protests. They ignore her, so she repeats the command more loudly. The rest of the riders know what is coming next. They all scatter, hoping not to be in the path of Abby's inevitable meltdown.

I decide to jump in before her voice can be read on the decibel scale, but by the time I step across the room, it is too late. Abby is screaming.

Her face is red, and her eyebrows are scrunched up so tightly they almost meet in the middle. Her voice is curdling; the hairs on the back of my neck are standing up, and my ears are scrunching from the sound. I am sure the sound contains words, but I cannot recognize any of them.

I lay my hand gently on her shoulder. I say, "Abby, what is the problem, and how can I help you?"

She retells the scene I have just witnessed with great drama and gasps for breath. But then she says something new: "They have to do what I say. I need them to do what I say."

There's a new thought. I had never seen it quite like that before. She *needs* them to do what she says. This is not just a desire with her. She doesn't simply like to be bossy; she has a *need* for people to do what she says.

"Abby, you are a leader, and leaders need someone to follow them. You needed your friends to follow your instructions." Her eyes light up in victory as she assumes that I will make all the riders get back on the bus. Then I continue: "But Abby, your words were not polite. They were bossy. People do not like to follow someone who is being bossy. They liked playing your bus game, but sometimes you need to let them decide what they want to do." She looks as if she is starting to get it.

"I will play bus. You can be the driver, and we will practice using nice words instead of bossy words." We practice several times. Other children come to join us. They follow my modeling. If they do not like the tone that Abby uses with them, they politely say, "I want to play with you. Could you say that in a nice way?" If Abby does not know what to say, I give her an example.

It takes a lot of practice on this first day, and we practice more on other days. Slowly, it becomes habit for her. Abby is on her way to becoming a great leader.

Accept Every Child's Characteristics as Positive

It was easy to get Abby's parents onboard with teaching her how to be a leader; they, too, enjoyed the reduction in ear-curdling volume. They were greatly relieved that I saw their daughter as a person with talent, not as a loud, bossy, spoiled child. By accepting Abby as the leader she is and building on those characteristics, we opened many doors in her future. If we had arranged a plan of punishment for her bossiness, she would have condemned herself and her true abilities. She would have ultimately been ashamed of what made her so great.

Children who express stubbornness have the talent of determination. Children who seem bossy may be untrained leaders. A child who is often quiet will one day have great thoughts. And the child who is hyper-organized will one day organize great things. If we condemn these traits because they seem to be negative behaviors, we may hinder the potential of the child discovering his or her own talents. Not all antisocial behavior is a sign of talent, but we need to be open to and aware of the possibility. Just as learning to eat starts out messy, talents can also be a bit unpleasant to begin with.

Do you remember a time when you were not given a choice? Maybe it was an art project that you had to do whether you liked it or not. I remember several writing assignments I struggled with in high school. Writing without a good cause just seemed like a waste of time. Whatever the circumstances, I am betting those memories are not the warm and fuzzy ones. They usually hold resentment and even anger. I believe that we should encourage children to try new things. But as a teacher you hold great power, and using that power to insist that children participate in an activity that they do not choose will not have a positive outcome. Providing each unique child with learning activities that suit his personality is a challenge, but it is one we should meet.

Reflection

Abby was the one who gave me the information I needed to help her. She also gave me a gift—a way of seeing children in a whole new light. I no longer viewed antisocial behavior as an issue that needs correction, but as an opportunity to see what the real problem is and teach the child what she needs to fix it. Abby's need to lead was not just a want or even a desire; it was a core need in her life. It was part of her very essence, in some ways just as much a need of hers as food was. She wouldn't physically suffer if we did not acknowledge her need to lead, but if life is not given the right environment to grow, it will eventually wilt and fade away.

Learning to see people's talents regardless of age takes practice. Sometimes talents are hidden deep inside. But looking for talent gives you a new appreciation for people in general. We can't all be the same. We can't all be the pitcher; we need outfielders and first basemen to play a game of baseball. In life, we need everyone and their talents to make it all work.

Watch your room for that hidden leader with bossy tendencies. I bet you will find her quickly if you don't already know who she is. I bet you can see the organizer and the artist. Let them learn and thrive in their talents, and help them to smooth out the rough edges.

Searching for Talents

1. Designate a time for each of the children's talents and intelligence to be developed during the normal flow of the day. Plan at least one opportunity a week per child, depending on how much

time they are with you during the day and the number of children in your class. Examples: Let Abby lead one group playtime with the goal of learning to give directions kindly. Ask Manuel to create one piece of artwork to display in the foyer.

2. Don't leave yourself out. Plan your day so that you have your own opportunities to develop your talents and abilities. You will find that you enjoy your day more and will be more effective as a teacher if you include yourself in the planning.

3. Ask a teacher who has a talent you do not have to participate in your class by meeting a need that you find difficult. Example: I would ask a teacher to tell a flannelboard story. This would add an area to my class that I cannot provide.

Suggested Reading

Hyson, Marilou. 2008. *Enthusiastic and engaged learners: Approaches to learning in the early childhood classroom.* New York: Teachers College Press.

10

New Shoes

Ashley has new shoes. She shows me the moment she walks in.

"Do you like my new shoes?" She skids to a stop.

"Wow, you are having fun in your new shoes!" I acknowledge.

Then I watch as she repeats the same question to everyone who enters the room. When Kate comes in with her mom, she asks Kate and Kate's mom. They reply with the normal responses: "I like your new shoes" or "Those are great new shoes." She smiles with pride.

She asks the group of boys playing in the construction area, "Do you like my new shoes?" They respond like boys in a construction area: "Yeah." She walks away with her head held high.

She approaches me again. "Do you like my new shoes?" This is odd, and I want to watch her more to figure out what is really going on.

"I can tell *you* really like your new shoes." I evade a direct answer again.

Just then the assistant director, Amy, comes in. "Do you like my new shoes?" Ashley inquires.

"Of course," Amy confirms.

A few more kids join our group—every time Ashley asks the same question and hears the same answers. Each time I see her pleased with the replies that they all like her new shoes.

Once more, very timidly this time, she asks me, "Do you like my shoes?"

What is she really asking me, and why is it so important to her that everyone acknowledge and like her new shoes? Could it be that she has connected personal acceptance and self-value to her new shoes? She is a remarkably striking little girl. She has dark brown curls with golden streaks and bright green eyes that make you look at her twice. She is dressed from a boutique, always concerned about her appearance. Other parents often comment on how beautiful she is; you can't help but notice. It is frightening to think that even at a young age she needs others' acknowledgment of her new shoes to feel liked by her peers.

"Why do you ask me again?" I look her squarely in the eyes.

"Because—do you like my shoes?" she says, looking down at the floor, afraid that I might say no.

"Ashley, I like you. I like you a lot, but not because of your shoes. I like the way you light up a room with your smile every day, and I like the way you are a good friend to those in our class. I like the way you always are polite, and I like your tender heart. That has nothing to do with what you put on your feet."

Still staring at her shoes and fidgeting, she is not satisfied with my answer.

So I call everyone over to group time. We sit in a circle. I ask each child to say his or her name loud and clear. We go around the circle stating our names—our names declare who we are. Then I go around the circle and make a statement about each child. Jarod is a great thinker. Kate is very compassionate. Erin is a unique artist. Ashley has a very tender heart. I continue until we are back to me. Then I have the children all take off their shoes and toss them into the center of the circle.

I ask them if they have changed at all. Is Jarod still a great thinker? Is Kate still compassionate? They laugh at first at the silly question. Then when it is Ashley's turn, I ask her, "Ashley, do you still have a tender heart?"

The light bulb goes on. "Yes," she says gently.

"Ashley, I *like* your tender heart."

After we finish this exercise about who we really are, I talk again with Ashley. "Ashley, new shoes are fun. I like when I get new shoes too. But I don't make friends because of my shoes, and it doesn't change who I am because I have new shoes. What is really important are the choices you make, what you like, what kind of friend you are, and who you decide to be." She nods, we hug, and she goes off to play, every once in a while still smiling at her new shoes.

I am not sure she gets it until her mom comes to pick her up. When Mom walks in the door, Ashley's face lights up. She runs and jumps into her arms and proclaims, "Today I have a new tender heart!" She gives Mom a hug.

"Yes, you do." She hugs back.

Give Compliments that Really Matter

Our culture has said that what you wear does define or, at minimum, reflect who you are. This saddens me greatly. What about those who cannot afford to dress to reflect? I do not want children's feelings of self-worth to be based on what I think about their shoes. I do not want them to define our relationship based on my approval of their new coats.

We want to acknowledge children and make them feel good, and appearance is the first thing we see. Noticing only appearance is a hard habit to break. We tell children that we like what they are wearing. We pay attention to the cute little girls or the spunky little boys. It takes a deeper relationship to recognize the child who is living inside the new shoes or the expensive jeans.

Acknowledging children based solely on their accomplishments can be equally dangerous. The children who gain self-worth from how they perform will become the driven workaholics of the future. They only feel valuable when they are accomplishing great things. The values of family or community will take a second place to the value of what they can accomplish. They become driven at all costs.

The value of people should be based on who they are—on their personalities, their preferences, and their talents. Just being who you are is valuable enough to be appreciated and respected as a person.

I am not saying that we shouldn't acknowledge the beauty. Nor should we ignore accomplishment. It is important to acknowledge and appreciate these things. What I am saying is not to make these things the cornerstone of your acknowledgment. Take the time to know a person on a deeper level. The following story tells how I myself reaped the benefits of someone acknowledging me on a deeper level.

The store clerk said I looked great this morning. I enjoyed the compliment for a moment, but it was quickly replaced with the business of getting to work, which included a phone call from my husband inviting me to lunch. On occasion my husband and I are lucky enough to enjoy lunch together. This was one of those lucky days. We ate at my favorite restaurant. Its lighting hides all those facial flaws that come with age. I was retelling one of the morning's adventures with a toddler when I noticed he was staring at me with a silly grin. I figured I had a piece of misplaced salad on my nose or something and he was just trying not to laugh. Instead he commented on the sparkle in my eyes when I talk about kids. He said he loves the way I love children. It makes him smile and remember the fun in life. That meant so much to me. I replayed his words throughout the day; they made my heart smile.

Two compliments: both were nice, but they were very different. The first was a statement of observation from an acquaintance. It was kind, and I appreciated it, but I soon forgot it. The other was powerful, never forgotten. What made the difference? It's simple: relationship.

The grocery clerk and I were acquaintances; we saw each other occasionally, enough for her to know that I didn't always look great. She had probably seen me in sweats and tennis shoes with my hair quickly pulled up and placed in a hair binder. Our relationship was superficial; we only knew each other's names because we read them on name tags and bank cards. My husband and I, thankfully, have a much deeper relationship. I know the story behind his name, and he knows never to call me by my legal first name. He sees me for who I really am; he knows the deeper me. He has seen me look my worst and my best, but what he appreciates in me is my personality, my belief system, and my values. He knows I have a talent for working with children, and that deep in my heart is a great love for them. He appreciates and enjoys me.

It is a common practice in our society to acknowledge the bright, the new, and the beautiful. But the dangers of this are very real. It gives children a value system that reinforces the idea that the beautiful and rich are better than those who are not. Children begin to think that new shoes are important—more important than who they are as persons, the choices they make, or the use of their talents.

Materialism has become the basis for judging ourselves, our community, and our world. I know that it is everywhere, in the media and so on. But we have the opportunity to break the cycle, to put value back into people, to change America's culture one child at a time.

Reflection

It has always bugged me a little when children ask the "Do you like my . . . ?" question. They ask if I like their art or if I like their hair. It is important to acknowledge what is important to them, but I wish my opinion didn't matter so much. Ashley's story gave me some insight into why these questions bother me. The children assign value to my opinions, when it is their own opinions that I want to highlight and acknowledge. Now my answers bring the attention to where it should be: to them. I often answer, "I am glad you are enjoying your new haircut." or "I can tell you like to use the color green." An even better response is to ask them questions so they can share their story. This shows that I truly am interested in them and that *they* are what I value.

It is natural to enjoy beautiful things. A study once reported that even babies prefer to look at photos of beautiful faces rather than not-so-beautiful ones. But materialism discards the person and elevates the materials.

In a school-age group I was with over spring break, I was tired of the name calling and judgmental statements that had overcome their friendships. So we took big white stickers and wrote positive descriptive words and wore them as name tags. So instead of calling Jamal by his given name, we called him Great Builder. Anna was Helper, and so on. When they couldn't remember the new given name, they would call their friends by whatever descriptive word they recognized in that child. For example, when they couldn't remember Anna was Helper, they would call her Smiley Girl. The attitude in the room changed in one short day.

Think about the last time you gave a child a compliment. What did you really say to the child?

Giving Sincere Compliments

1. Tell parents of their child's uniqueness. Not only will this build your relationship with parents, but it may just open their eyes as well.
2. Build a display of the children's "true colors." Use stories or photos of children expressing their personalities.
3. Build children's skills. Use activities to enhance, practice, and perfect each child's uniqueness.

Suggested Reading

Kaufman, Gershen, Lev Raphael, and Pamela Espeland. 1999. *Stick up for yourself! Every kid's guide to personal power and positive self-esteem.* Rev. and updated ed. Minneapolis: Free Spirit Publishing.

Roberts, Rosemary. 2006. *Self-esteem and early learning: Key people from birth to school.* 3rd ed. London: Paul Chapman Publishing.

PART THREE

Help Me Learn in New Ways

11

Mistaken Behavior

There are probably as many different routines for dealing with lunch plates in preschool classrooms as there are preschool classrooms that serve lunch. Every teacher has a system of how children clear their plates after lunch. Each child learns where to put the silverware, what to throw away, and what not to. It will depend on where they eat, how the food is served, and how it is disposed of. The routine keeps the process safe and sanitary. But even with a routine there are always mishaps.

I remember one of those days quite clearly. I had designed a workable system:

Stand up and push in your chair.
Reach for your plate.
Take it to the fifty-five-gallon garbage pail.
Use the scraper to scrape off any remaining food.
Put the plate in the bin.
Return the scraper to the holder for the next child.

It was a successful routine, and things usually ran smoothly. But today, Jada forgets to shove in her chair. This leads to a domino effect of slop. Jada walks to the garbage, but Jerry isn't so lucky. His right foot gets caught in her chair and jolts his steps enough to wiggle the plate of leftover mashed potatoes, gravy, and peas loose into Kim's hair and onto the floor. Kim immediately jumps up, knocking Jerry backward into Joe's path so that now Jerry gets to wear Joe's leftovers. The normal cries erupt. Jada has turned in time to see the dominoes fall, and she knows who knocked over the first one. She freezes. My assistant goes to make sure no one is seriously injured, and I step toward Jada.

"Wow, that's some mess!" I want to give her the opportunity to talk about how she is feeling. "What do you think we should do?"

Other children are beginning to look at her and place blame.

"It wasn't me. I sat over there." She points to an unoccupied table. Of course this is met with strong resistance from every child in the room.

After encouraging the children to return to their meal, I once again approach Jada, who has gone to the area she had claimed as her spot and is fighting back tears.

"Jada, I forget to do stuff all the time. Remember yesterday, when I forgot to pour the milk for lunch?"

"Yeah, you were silly."

"Yep, and sometimes I forget to close the door when we go to gym, and it gets so cold in here. Do you remember that?"

"Yeah, we put on our coats for a while."

"Everybody makes mistakes, and it feels awful when we do. But I know how to make it better. You have to fix your mistakes. When I forgot the milk, I had to stop eating my own lunch and get up and get the milk ready for you all. And we had to wear our coats inside because I forgot to close the door. I made mistakes, and I fixed them, and I felt better. Did you make a mistake today?"

It takes awhile, but Jada finally admits to forgetting about the chair, apologizes to her classmates, and helps me clean up the floor and chairs.

When we are done, we talk about how much nicer it is to fix our mistakes than to lie and have everyone yell at us.

It is important to reassure her that my job is to help her when she makes mistakes. Then she will feel confident in approaching me for help, rather then fearing punishment.

"I promise if you ever need help fixing a mistake, I will be here to help you. All of your teachers will help when you need us."

A few days later, Jada's mom comes to talk with me. "Miss Cindylee, apparently I am supposed to talk with you." My face expresses my confusion; I don't remember sending a note or anything. "Jada said that I made her wear her dress shoes to church yesterday, and that was a *big mistake*, and that you are supposed to help me with my mistake and make me feel better about it." Thankfully, she says this with a big grin.

Think of Mistakes as Learning Opportunities

I felt good when I got through to Jada after the post-lunch mess. I felt even better when her mom confirmed to me that the lesson had stuck. That just goes to show what the central message of Jada's story is. Mistakes are great! They don't necessarily feel great, but they are one of my favorite teaching tools. Making mistakes develops character. Think of all the lessons that can come from making mistakes. Here are a few:

Perseverance	Determination
Self-awareness	Resolve
Self-acceptance	Awareness of others
Forgiveness	Problem-solving
Tolerance	And sometimes, just plain cause and effect

Mistakes do not need to be punished or condemned; they need to be used as teaching opportunities. If a child makes a mistake, then that child needs to learn how to fix it. Many of life's lessons are learned through making mistakes:

If you make a mess, clean it up.
If you accidentally trip someone, step on her toes, bump into her, etc., tell her you are sorry and help her up.
If your first attempt doesn't work, try again.
Never give up.
Practice makes perfect.

If we choose to look at antisocial behavior as mistakes instead of misbehavior, our response to the behavior will change. Unlike misbehavior requiring punishment or reprimands, mistaken behavior requires teaching. This change of thought can revolutionize your stress level. As a teacher you will no longer be doling out punishment; instead, you can spend your time teaching children positive, socially acceptable behavior. Teaching children how to fix their mistakes will enable them to develop strong relationships, build the confidence they need to solve their own problems, and give them a feeling of ability instead of powerlessness.

Children will often resort to dishonesty to avoid the guilt and condemnation that come as a result of being punished for mistakes. They will lie to get out of trouble, even to the point that they believe the lie themselves. As a teacher you need to help them face their mistakes, accept responsibility, and bring them to a positive resolution. This will eliminate the fear of punishment, and children will begin to face their problems with the confidence they need to fix them.

Jada's story is about an accident. She did not leave her chair out on purpose; it was not a thought-out, purposeful act. On the other hand, I have watched a child think, walk up to another child, and slap that child across the face. This is an unprovoked act of aggression and violence. This action involves two mistakes—the thought and the slap—but it is still a mistake. Even premeditated misbehavior is a mistake. Anger is a secondary, responsive emotion. It usually comes as a response to being hurt. First we are hurt, and then we get mad. The emotions are not a mistake, but the behavior of retaliation is. In order to provide a resolution, we must deal with not only the slap, but the cause of the hurt that moved this child to strike back.

Dan Gartrell has written many great books about mistaken behavior, including *A Guidance Approach for the Encouraging Classroom* (2006). He divides behaviors into three different levels—experimentation, socially influenced, and strong needs. My experiences have led me to name these a bit differently. I define the three levels of mistaken behavior as: cause-and-effect, social behavior, and unmet needs. Jada's story is a perfect example of a cause-and-effect mistake. She left her chair out, and the effect was an accident. My son Jason threw a Duplo through a window when he was two. After I heard the crash, I ran to the play room, and there he stood, totally in shock. His mouth was even hanging open. His eyes were twice their normal size, and when he saw me, he just pointed to the window. Windows weren't supposed to do that! He was stunned. This was purely a cause-and-effect mistake. He threw the Duplo, and the old window broke. Then he had a problem. When children trip and bump someone, when they throw a ball and their lack of skill sends the ball into their friend's back, when they play with a toy and it breaks—these are all examples of cause-and-effect mistakes. They need to be addressed. The child needs to take responsibility and come to a resolution. This is how children learn that even though these actions were beyond their control, they still need to take responsibility and fix the problem. It's the same situation as when our car slides on ice into another vehicle; we are still responsible for the accident.

Social behavior mistakes are problems between people. It doesn't take long in a preschool classroom to see what this means. One of the most common examples goes like this: "He took my toy so I slugged him (or grabbed it back)." Social behavior mistakes illustrate a lack of training in social skills. Children have to learn how to be good friends, how to draw boundaries, and how to respond when someone crosses the line.

This reminds me of my personal pet peeve. Bear with me while I share. I hate the use of lines in preschool classrooms! Who goes first, who is last, who budged in, who bumped who, I want to be by her . . . Ugh! Preschool lines cause more problems than they cause order. Avoid them whenever possible. I've liked to have my classes go places as a group. They learned to pay attention to where they were going. There were no hurt feelings because someone never got to go first. There were no crushed feelings because someone was last. Children do eventually learn to stand in lines, but this happens when they are older and have had more social practice. Try doing away with lines for a month. You'll like it!

The third level of mistaken behavior, unmet-needs mistakes, are behaviors that have a deeper level of cause. A child who has an unmet need acts out in an attempt to get the need met. A child who only gets attention when she misbehaves will continue the process of mistaken behavior to meet her attention need. If a child does not feel as if he is in control over what happens to him, he will act out just to feel as if he has some say in his own life. This type of behavior is common in children whose parents are constantly rushing off to work, dragging the children around in order not to be late. The children don't get to choose what to eat, what to wear, where to sit in the car, or even the pace at which they walk. These children will look for opportunities to express power in any way they can. *Any* person who doesn't feel a sense of control over her circumstances feels belittled and valueless. Sometimes the resulting behavior does not readily point at a cause. The child may have a need without any clue about how to get it met. The child could act with aggression; withdraw from relationships; be overly energetic, running around the room disrupting anyone and everyone; or become lethargic and refuse to participate.

Unmet-needs mistakes have to be treated at the source. We don't ignore the responsibility for the behavior. Children are still responsible for the resulting offenses. But to truly help these children we need to help them realize why they are expressing mistaken behavior, and then we need to figure out how to properly get their needs met. If we don't, they will just try the behavior again and again until the need is met.

Behaviors do not always fall into one certain category. One example is hitting. Hitting someone because you tripped over your own feet and your hand just flew up is a cause-and-effect mistake. The resolution would be to apologize and try to make the other person feel better. Hitting a classmate because she said mean words to you is a socially mistaken behavior. We need to teach that child to tell the classmate that those are mean words. Hitting because a child is stressed when his parents are getting a divorce is an unmet-needs mistaken behavior. The resolution may take time, as we help the child and parents to deal with their emotions of loss and stress.

I often get asked, "What about teaching children choices and consequences?" Here's my answer.

It depends on how you teach it. Are you the enforcer of consequences? Do you *tell* the child what to do, or do you come alongside the child to help him deal with the consequences that already exist? Teachers are responsible for setting boundaries and behavioral expectations. When we don't want children running in the classroom, we ask them to walk. When we don't want children hitting each other, we teach them to ask for their toy back. Then we make sure that it works. If children use their words instead of their hands, we need to make sure that their words are effective. If they ask for their toy and it isn't returned, they will resort to using their hands again.

Helping a Child through Mistaken Behavior

1. Define the mistaken behavior and its level. (See the What and Why chart on page 83 for help with this.)
2. Help the child take responsibility and make resolution for the mistake.

3. Help the child discover the socially acceptable behavior.

4. Follow through; make sure the new behavior works effectively.

I wanted to introduce these concepts to parents, so I made a huge poster with these steps printed on it. Then I hung it in my room where I could see it and where parents could see it. Some parents wanted their own copy, so I made smaller posters they could take with them for their own use. Time and time again they returned with stories of success. Their relationship with their child was more pleasant. They felt this process had revolutionized their parenting, and they were incredibly satisfied with the results. They had a greater level of enjoyment when interacting with their children.

Reflection

My moments with Jada solidified my thoughts about mistaken behavior. I was just in the process of discovering how children face punishment when this story took place. Prior to the lunchtime dominoes, I had been a disciplinarian more then a teacher. I responded to children's behavior by telling them what they had done wrong and what would be the consequences of their choices. After this event, I realized there is a core connection between fear of taking responsibility and fear of being judged and punished.

How do you feel when you have made a mistake? Is your first reaction to fix it, or do you suffer from the "It wasn't me" complex? Our responses are generally formed from previous experiences mixed with a chunk of our personality. Some children have a high sense of empathy, and the thought that they may have hurt someone else is almost more than they can bear. These children would rather lie or hide than face the truth. How do the children in your care respond to mistakes? How will you help them solve them and learn from them?

One of the tools I use to help myself define which level of behavior I am dealing with is a What and Why chart. I share it with you here.

A Child of What Age Did What and Why?

A five-year-old hit because someone stepped on her shoelace and she fell, hitting someone on the way down.

This is a cause-and-effect behavior. Make sure everyone is okay, then help the child apologize, and learn more about making sure everyone's shoes are tied.

A four-year-old hit because someone took his toy.

This is a social behavior that needs to be resolved, and new behavior needs to be taught.

A three-year-old hit because she was tired and someone got in her way.

This is an unmet need behavior. Make sure that there are no serious injuries. Remind the child that hitting is not okay, that asking people to move is, and then meet the need and help her get some sleep. We might talk with parents to see if bedtimes need to be adjusted if this is an ongoing issue. If it's a one-time issue, then naptime will solve it.

Suggested Reading

Bilmes, Jenna. 2004. *Beyond behavior management: The six life skills children need to thrive in today's world.* Saint Paul: Redleaf Press.

Evans, Betsy. 2002. *You can't come to my birthday party! Conflict resolution with young children.* Ypsilanti, MI: High/Scope Press.

12

The Recipe Book

I pride myself on having a language-rich classroom. There are books in every area, writing utensils and paper everywhere. The block area has graph paper so little construction workers can develop blueprints. I bought decorative paper pads for lists in the home living area along with several recipe cards and recipe books. The children enjoy many opportunities for hands-on literacy learning.

On this day, it is time to prepare for lunch. Each child is returning classroom items to their designated spots. Steve and Kevin are demolishing the block neighborhood they created and returning the blocks to the shelves. Jessica, Mariah, and David are watching the colors run off their paintbrushes and blend together before disappearing down the sink drain. Zeke returns the counters to the shelf to await the next time they will get to come out and play. Jada is assigned the task of kitchen helper, so she and I are setting the tables for the coming feast. Karrin comes to me with one of the recipe books in her hand and a puzzled look on her face. "Miss Cindylee, this book has pictures of food in it, so does it go in the reading area? It has numbers too, so does it go in the science area?"

"What are the pictures of?" I want her to figure it out on her own.

"Well, there are some dinners. But there are some measuring cups like in the water table, but we don't put books in water. They get mushy." That had been demonstrated a few days earlier.

It is important for children to use the keys from the room to be able to know where things belong. I want her to feel successful at solving her own problems, so I continue to present questions that I hope will give her the answers she is looking for. "Where in the class would we find things to make dinner?"

"On the lunch table. We don't have books at the lunch tables." She shakes her head as if she is informing me of the rule.

Sometimes, we just need to show children the answer so that they can get it next time. "Karrin, that is a recipe book. We use it in the home living area when we want to cook food. Would you please put it in the home living area?"

She smiles and says, "Cool cookies."

Cool cookies? Did she say "cool cookies"? That's what I always say! It is strange to hear it come out of a preschooler's mouth. She even drew out the word "cooool," the same way I do. In fact, Karrin sounded like a little me. I say "cool cookies" as an affirmation, like many say "okay" or "okey dokey." I say it many times a day without thinking about it. Karrin used it in the exact same context in which I use it. My eyes follow her to the home living kitchen, where she sits the book upright on top of the little table. She carefully sets the hard book covers apart to balance the book, then she fans the pages to finish the nice look, just the way I would have done.

I look around at my room. Kenny G's smooth jazz sax is drifting in the background. The boys have asked assistance from Jessica to help them put the Legos in the big yellow basket, and the blocks are back on the shelves, arranged by color and size. The children are finishing by lining up the trucks against the wall. The trucks are facing outward, as if they are about to take off, rather than as if they have just been parked. The mosquito netting above the reading area makes it look inviting and adds a comfy touch. Illustrated book covers are collaged on one wall, and puppets on a shelf create the other wall. I am at home. It feels good here. The kids are engaged; there's noise in the room, but it somehow sounds peaceful. There is even a vanilla scent drifting by my nose. I like being here. We like being here. We belong here.

Create the Right Environment

At that moment, everything we had been working on finally fell into place. It had just happened. The room arrangement was perfect and effective. The children trusted me to meet their needs and to be available when they needed me. They knew when they came in the door that something fun would happen with all of us, that they would be challenged to try something new, that they would be introduced to something they hadn't seen or hadn't thought of yet. Friendships would blossom and grow.

The room was comfortable and homey yet engaging. It called you into it. It wanted you to see all that it had to offer. New tools in the Artist Arena waited to be tried. There were stories that needed to be read and magnifying glasses that yearned to show you a closer look. Towns waited to be constructed; space vehicles longed to be invented. The yellow cardboard bus we had created beckoned the children to board it. Colored bears of different sizes needed to be weighed and measured. Music waited to be conducted. The room needed us; we needed it. And we needed each other.

It was evident that I wasn't the only one who was comfortable in the room. The children were interacting with the environment with purpose and ease. Karrin had even picked up the slang that I use. When many people live together, they begin to know the language, the routines, and the expectations of the group. It is all part of the environment. I remember one Christmas when my brother came to my home. He was wrapping presents for the upcoming celebration. He was trying to find the tape, and I had told him, "It's in the drawer." He had no clue which drawer I was referring to. There were drawers all over the house—in both bathrooms, every bedroom, the kitchen, the hallway, and the garage. Which drawer could possibly be *the* drawer? My daughter took his hand and guided him to the kitchen, where she introduced "the drawer" and its normal contents. My daughter and I had spent four years together. We spoke the same drawer language; we shared the same environment.

What makes a preschool environment? Mary Renck Jalongo and Joan Isenberg define it in *Exploring Your Role* (2000, 149): "By *environment*, we mean the combination of a planned arrangement of physical space, the relationships between and among the people, and the values and goals of a particular program, center, or school system. Environment is the sum total of these influences that affect particular individuals and groups of people. Yet each environment is unique because of how these influences interact."

In other words, the environment includes room arrangement and contents, the children and the teacher, and the values or goals that you have for the program. These elements combined are what create the classroom environment.

There are plenty of resources that can help you have a balanced, effective room arrangement. I list a few at the end of this chapter. A good room arrangement does not always mean a successful classroom, but a bad arrangement can ensure that you have an ineffective room. If a class is struggling, room arrangement is usually the first thing to take a look at.

The children and their personalities and the teachers with their personalities, combined with the goals of the program, are vital parts of an early learning environment. For several years I taught preschool in the same classroom with basically the same equipment, but each fall when a new group arrived, the room seemed to change. One year I had quite a rambunctious group. They were very physical and loud. When we sat in a group, they looked like a bunch of jumping beans unable to contain their energies. I added a climber to the room to meet their need for a lot of physical activity. The ambience was always fun and exciting. The next year my group was softer and thrived in a quieter room with solid routines. The climber seemed like a waste of space.

As children live in classrooms, they become part of the environment. Children will acquire the same language, the same routines, and even the mannerisms of those around them. In the story, Karrin repeated my expression "cool cookies." She inherited that from spending time with me. She even had my tone down. I was suddenly aware of how powerful my impact was on the children in my group. They had learned to organize the classroom the way I determined was best. The room had my special touches right down to the music and the scent. We were a part of the learning environment, and I had a powerful part to play. The comfort level I felt at that time was purposefully planned. I had allowed my personality to take shape in the room, and that made it secure and snug for all.

Whenever I have served as a director, I can always tell when a new teacher decides to take ownership of the classroom. The teacher cleans out every cupboard, rearranges everything, changes things on the walls, and adds personal touches. This is an exciting time; it is when things really get good. The teacher becomes personally vested in the room and in the children who live there. She begins to take possession of the room and of her role in it. It reminds me of the effort that goes into creating a good baseball mitt. Mitts work well on the day you buy them, but they are kind of stiff. After a mitt gets broken in, it begins to form to the hand of the one who uses it. Then the owner uses a fluid to mold the glove around a ball. This makes the mitt truly effective. When a ball comes to the mitt, it falls right into place, snug and tight. The mitt is fulfilling its purpose, and the ball and the hand are comfortable with it. A teacher who molds his classroom around the children and provides the perfect fit for his hand has created an environment that is perfectly fit for those who use it.

The other quality needed to make a complete environment is the program's goals and values. When I put trucks in my block area, I face them out rather than having them look as if they are parked. Believe it or not, this is a demonstration of one of the assets I value in a room—it is engaging. A truck facing out looks ready to go, not as if it is all done. A book propped up and open is inviting a child to look at it. Mosquito netting in the reading area provides coziness. So do the throw pillows. These are all traits that I value—a room that is accessible, safe, interactive, and engaging. These qualities make an effective learning environment.

The goals for those of us teaching in that room were to educate, to engage, and to build up, and these goals were apparent when you looked around. Throughout the room you could see the children actively engaged in the learning processes, and it was an enjoyable experience for them. The far wall held our art exhibit. Each child had a frame and got to choose what was displayed in it. There were reference books they could use to get real answers to their questions. Our bus, which we named Jimmy, was waiting for us to join it. The children had seen their siblings get on a bus and wanted to create one for themselves, so we did. The room expressed their involvement and demonstrated their success at learning. Our program goals and values were worked out in the environment. We valued each individual child, and it showed. We valued the children's involvement, and it showed. We valued the learning process, and it showed.

The effects of the children, myself, the equipment, and the values of the program were obvious in the ambience of the classroom. Together we created a quality learning environment; together we made it work.

Reflection

When I stopped and looked around that day, it felt good to feel that I belonged. I was in a place where I knew I was safe. It was safe for me to be the person I was meant to be, a teacher. I was meant to provide a high quality, nurturing, early learning environment, and I was doing that. It was a "home run" feeling. All of my hard work, the planning, the preparing, the practicing, and the giving—it had all come together. I had hit a home run. Inside I was running the bases. I breathed deeply and had my own little mini-celebration moment. Except for moments with my own children, this was the most satisfied I have ever felt.

The classroom environment can create an atmosphere of learning, or it can create an atmosphere of chaos. Creating a positive learning environment is one of the teacher's biggest jobs. It is all-inclusive, and it is a make-or-break deal.

When you look at the three areas that make up the classroom environment—relationships, physical arrangement, and program values—how do you rate your effectiveness in creating a positive learning environment? Developing your desired environment takes time. It is an ever-evolving process, and any change can cause fluctuations. Add a new child to the group, and the dynamics can change quickly. But with patience, planning, and practice you will reach your own home run moment.

Suggested Reading

Curtis, Deb, and Margie Carter. 2003. *Designs for living and learning: Transforming early childhood environments.* Saint Paul: Redleaf Press.

Greenman, Jim. 2005. *Caring spaces, learning places: Children's environments that work.* Redmond, WA: Exchange Press.

Jalongo, Mary Renck, and Joan P. Isenberg. 2000. *Exploring your role: A practitioner's introduction to early childhood education.* Upper Saddle River, NJ: Merrill.

National Association for the Education of Young Children. 2007. *NAEYC early childhood program standards and accreditation criteria: The mark of quality in early education.* Washington, DC: NAEYC.

13

The Quiet One

Johnny is playing on the floor by himself. He is quietly creating a rainbow with colored dinosaurs. He puts all the red ones in one row and the purple ones in their own row. It is hard to know what Johnny is thinking during much of the day. He doesn't spend a lot of time talking or running around. His emotions don't seem to swing to the normal highs and lows that are typical in a preschool group; he is more controlled and steady. He is smart and sweet, but he does not like hugs and only on a rare occasion will he give a "high five."

I sit down, legs crossed and hands folded, and watch. Johnny's small hands move slowly, purposefully. Done with the purple row, he starts the green dino line in his rainbow. He picks up a green one, holds it for a moment, looks me squarely in the eyes, and hands it to me. He has given me permission to exist in his space, to participate in his world. I put it in the correct spot and pick up another. There are no words exchanged between us; he sees no use for them.

The rainbow grows. All loose dinos are put into their places, and our task is complete. He looks up at me again, and then his hand moves for the dinosaur container. It is his indication that our time is nearly done. The rainbow is tossed into the bucket, stirring up the colors again. His ending smile provides the closing, and off he goes.

Help Children Learn in Ways that Make Each of Them Comfortable

The relationship between Johnny and me had changed over time; our connective threads had grown stronger. The absence of words testified to the depth of our communication. We no longer needed to communicate on the surface to benefit from each other's presence; we could enjoy togetherness without the limitation of mere words.

This is the hardest task of all—spending pure time with children. During that playtime I gathered many valuable observations about Johnny's development that I added to his assessment portfolio. He was sorting and classifying, both important math skills. But the value of the relationship development was what struck me the most. He allowed me into his space because I waited for his invitation. Had I just sat down and jumped into his dino play, the response would have been drastically different. Knowing his typical responses, I believe he would have let me take over and then just left.

Respecting individuality is key to any relationship. Allowing children room to be themselves gives them the respect they deserve. Johnny does not enjoy being a part of large groups. He prefers to play with just one or two others at a time. I respect that and plan my day to create choices that fit Johnny's need to be in a small group. He can explore the same concepts that all the children have an opportunity to explore without being put into circumstances that make him uncomfortable. If I tried to force Johnny to participate in a large group event that he had not chosen, he would resent me. I would no longer have his trust.

At times I have asked Johnny to participate with me by his side. Because I have his trust and he has my respect, he has honored my request and reluctantly participated. I always thank him for his courageous attempt, but I do not push the point.

Every child has preferences and talents that need to be respected. No one benefits from being forced to do something. Don't get me wrong: we all have things in life that we have to do whether we like them or not, like eating vegetables. In a classroom there are routines we must follow. For example, we cannot let a child stay inside alone when the group is headed outdoors. But at every opportunity we need to give children the choice as to the level at which they would like to participate. There are always other options in which the child can have the same learning opportunity. We just have to be creative.

Many types of tools help us to define individual tendencies. One of the most commonly used in the educational field is Howard Gardner's multiple intelligences theory (2006). He recognizes eight different types of intelligences: linguistic, logical-mathematical, spatial, bodily-kinesthetic, musical, interpersonal, intrapersonal, and naturalist.

- Linguistic intelligence uses language to express ideas and to understand others. People who have verbal intelligence need to talk about things and debate. They love to read and write.
- Logical-mathematical intelligence uses reasoning to understand information. People with logical intelligence often enjoy graphing and organizing information into categories.
- Spatial intelligence uses images to understand information. People with visual intelligence like to see things; they often think in images rather than words.
- Bodily-kinesthetic intelligence uses movement to learn. People with kinesthetic intelligence like drama and games, and they must move even when listening to a story.
- Musical intelligence involves thinking in musical patterns. People with this type of intelligence like rhythm and listening for the

beat; they often hum or sing even when there is no other music around.

- Interpersonal intelligence uses relationships to learn. People with this type of intelligence like teamwork and do not function well on their own.
- Intrapersonal intelligence is internally reflective. People with this type of intelligence understand information as it relates to their being.
- Naturalist intelligence involves processing and organizing information from the observable world. People with naturalist intelligence are good at categorizing items, especially those in the natural world.

Johnny was a logical-mathematical learner. He wanted his world in order, and he took in new information by organizing it. He did not need to talk about it, the way a linguistic learner would, and he definitely did not enjoy working as part of a team, as someone with interpersonal intelligence would. He did have strong intrapersonal intelligence tendencies, but more often than not I found him organizing, classifying, and graphing. These habits reflect a logical intelligence.Understanding these categories of intelligence helps us to include all children's learning tendencies in our classroom. We want to make sure children have a variety of learning experiences, with information presented so that everyone can assimilate it.

Gardner helps us understand the different ways children understand information, but there are many aspects to individuality. At an early age children begin to reveal their personalities, talents, and abilities, and—if you look closely—their learning styles.

Reflection

Johnny's story is dear to my heart. I have learned to meet children's needs according to their styles rather than according to mine. It certainly is not my teaching style to sit quietly, not saying a word. I enjoy talking so much that there are days my throat starts to hurt from being over-used! Regardless of my style, it was Johnny's style that really mattered. Matching my teaching to his learning style was more important than my own self-expression. Teaching so that the child may learn is a greater goal than teaching for its own sake.

Take time on a regular basis to reflect upon the gifts, unique perspectives, and learning styles of each child in your care. Sometimes we become so focused on learning objectives that we forget to think carefully about the path that will help each child meet them. Sometimes we forget that everyone does not see and respond to the world as we do.

Remember to build observation time into each day. The children will show you how they prefer to learn if you give them the space and time to do so. How will you do that today? How will you give children their own piece of the day so that you can learn from them?

Suggested Reading

Wilford, Sara. 2009. *Nurturing Young Children's Disposition to Learn*. Saint Paul: Redleaf Press.

Will, Tamara J., Karen King, and Michelle Mergler. 2007. *Great preschools: Building developmental assets in early childhood*. Minneapolis: Search Institute.

14

Are We There Yet?

Once again, I call Teryn's mom at work and ask her to bring in some more dry clothes for her daughter. She brings a few sets every morning, but today we have already gone through them. Teryn's doctor has said that there is no physical reason that she isn't toilet trained; physically, everything is fine. She will celebrate her third birthday in two weeks, and her mom is desperate.

Without a word I hand Teryn's mom a heavy bag of wet clothes; her sigh is even heavier. We have tried many tricks of the trade. We have Teryn go potty every half hour; she sits, and we wait and wait and wait. My favorite was when Mom tried floating targets. They dissolve after about ten minutes of being wet, and the picture on the target turns into a cute bunny when urine hits it. That's what I heard anyway, because I never saw it happen. I can't think of any encouraging words that I haven't already said. In fact, I am beginning to sound like a broken record.

Finally I speak: "My children are ten, twelve, and seventeen. They are all potty trained." She gives me a sarcastic laugh as I continue. "I don't even remember what age they were potty trained. I know I went through a lot of agony with two of them, but I do know that this too will pass. Someday Teryn will be potty trained, I promise." It seemed to relieve a bit of her tension.

Think about What Each Child Is Ready to Learn

When? When is the right time to toilet teach a child? When is the right time for children to begin reading, or how high should they count when they are three years old? One of the most unusual "When . . . ?" questions I was asked by a parent was, "When should they be responsible for opening their own door?" I said, "What?" I wasn't sure I had heard the parent correctly.

What behavior and development should come at what ages is a question we have all been asking for years. The NAEYC book *Developmentally Appropriate Practice in Early Childhood Programs* (Copple and Bredekamp 2009) presents a fairly good picture. If you don't have a copy of this book available to you, find one. Buy it, or get it from the library. Even better, suggest that your boss buy a copy for you and everybody you work with. The book describes not only appropriate behavioral expectations in each age group but also inappropriate and appropriate teaching practices for that age group.

The most common question I have been asked as a preschool teacher is, "When do they start learning to read?" Here is my answer.

"Reading is just one part of being literate. Children need to have a firm grasp of a language and words before they can comprehend what they are reading or why they are reading. It really began at birth. When you talked with your infant, you were beginning to build a language base. When we introduce new words and information to children, we are giving them a broader base to draw from.

"If a second grader is reading in her reader and comes across the words 'fire hydrant,' it will take her seven times of reading those words in context before she has a comprehension of what she is reading. But if that child went on a walk with us when she was in preschool, and we saw a fire hydrant, touched it, talked about it, and looked at where the firefighters hook up their hoses, the first time she reads 'fire hydrant,' she will have immediate comprehension. If we are spending our time trying to get children to write a perfect letter F, they will miss out on the walk.

"Before children can learn to read, they need to learn that what they say can be written down, and that what is written down can be said. They need to learn that reading goes from left to right and top to bottom and that a book goes from front to back. Writing is another piece of literacy. It is more than being able to make letters; it requires a different set of tools. Children must have command over the muscles in their fingers. Coloring and painting build the muscles that will be used for writing. Being exposed to the many different ways we use the written language in real life gives a child cause to want to write. That is why you see pencils in our kitchen area—so children can write their own shopping lists or recipe cards. That is why there is graph paper in the construction area. Literacy is a complex process. Every day we complete many tasks that will build your child's comprehension, reading abilities, and writing abilities." It's a long answer, I know. But it is true, and the theory I described works.

Some areas in early childhood research and knowledge seem to swing from one extreme to the other. The age at which you begin feeding an infant solid food is one of those topics. Twenty years ago, when my children were infants, we started them on solids at around eight weeks. About five years later, pediatricians recommended no solid foods of any kind until a child was a year old. That was a bad idea, but it was what their studies showed to be the best at the time. Currently, the thought is that it is best to begin to introduce solids to infants at about six months. Child development is an ever-changing and evolving field. New studies support new and better ways every year. For the most part this research has changed our profession into one of true quality and merit. We continue to adapt program guidelines and procedures based on the best information that is available to us at that moment. I have seen televisions leave classrooms, yet at one time they were used to help children take naps. Brain research began to give a clearer picture of what television really does to the brain. It exercises the part of the brain that controls basic instincts and survival mechanisms; it does not use the thinking part of the brain. I want to build the thinking parts of children's brains.

I have seen worksheets leave the room, and now I have seen them trickling back in again. The new awareness of the importance of kindergarten readiness has caused some programs to include them again. Children are learning literacy at a younger age in order to properly prepare them for the more advanced learning of kindergarten. Our preschools are beginning to look like my children's kindergarten programs eighteen years ago. Time will tell if this is a positive change, but for now we act on the best information that we have available to us.

Children vary in what age they start learning to read. I had one student, Jack, who was at a second-grade reading level when he went off to kindergarten. He had a natural gift and a strong desire to read. Since he was interested, we provided him with the knowledge he desired and many opportunities to explore language. The results were amazing. Here is one of his stories.

It was springtime, and with spring always come spring sports. In many states children can begin to participate in organized sports when they are four years old. Jack had just turned four and was ready to begin his sporting career. The morning after his first T-ball practice, he entered the classroom with a new metal T-ball bat. He ran straight up to me with a sparkle in his eyes. His mouth was full of words; he could hardly get them out fast enough. My initial response was to ignore his words and latch on to the bat with full force, but he was holding it harmlessly by the neck, vertically. I decided that if it went horizontal, it was mine.

He opened his mouth to pour out words. I concentrated on listening and keeping my eyes on his eyes, not on the bat. The bat was still visible, though. I am fanatical about safety, but there was no immediate threat, and so I forced myself to listen to his words. " Yesterday was my first day at sports camp . . ." Then I heard his friends' names. I heard how far he hit the ball. I heard his coach's name. Then I heard the name of his bat. He pointed to the letters on his bat. "S, L, U, G, G, E, R, Slugger," he said, as he sounded them out. Then, beaming, very loudly and clearly he said: "I did it *all by myself*."

His mouth was now empty, and he was grinning from ear to ear. The punch line had been delivered—he had sounded out the name all by himself. It was what I was supposed to notice and acknowledge. I did so with pride, and I asked him if he wanted to find more words. We put the bat in a safe place. Then we spent an entire hour reading words, sometimes with other children, sometimes just the two of us.

Not every child is ready to read at four years old, but Jack is a gifted child, and he is advanced in many areas of development. He can beat me at checkers every time, even when I try to beat him. It's embarrassing!

Had I gone with my first instinct and freaked out about a metal bat in my classroom full of children, I would have ruined the moment. Jack would have abided by my wishes and removed the bat from the room, but I would have missed the golden opportunity to connect with Jack, to spend a glorious hour of scaffolding, connecting neurons, developing self-esteem, and smiling.

He had something to tell me. It wasn't about the sports camp or his teammates—that was just the setup. It was about his reading. By telling his story, he was letting me know that he wanted to learn more letters and how they were put together to form familiar words.

Children will often tell us what they really need if we take the time to listen. We want them to follow our plans and to accomplish our agendas, but if we take the time to listen, we will hear what is meaningful and valuable to them. If it is meaningful and valuable, they will remember it. They will use it, and they will learn more than we had planned.

A child once said to me, "You couldn't tell me if I didn't want to know." It wasn't a confrontational statement. He said it in a matter-of-fact voice, but he had realized that unless he wanted to know about something, he wouldn't retain the information I was giving him. He said it perfectly.

That is your answer. It is time to teach a child to read when that child wants to read. You can create an environment that gives a child curiosity about reading and plenty of opportunities to try it out. When a child is big enough to open his own door and it is safe, that child will do it if you don't. You can give a child the opportunity to get toilet trained, and when she is ready—physically, emotionally, and motivationally—it will happen. I promise.

As teachers, we provide the optimal learning environment. We give children the tools and the opportunities. We encourage them to try. We can set up the environment to stir up curiosity, and when they want to know it, they will learn it. That is the right time to teach them.

Reflection

This year my youngest son will be eighteen, and I will become a mom of all adult children. I can hardly remember the Little League days, let alone the toileting days. When you are in that moment that Teryn's mom was experiencing, you don't think anything will ever change. But in truth, it all goes by so fast. The right information at the right time is important. The right information at the wrong time can feel frustrating and fruitless.

Have you had experiences when you have told children information several times, but then, at that right moment, they get it—I mean, really get it? The light bulb goes on, and they remember it. They take ownership of the information and even incorporate it into other areas. For whatever reason, at that moment they needed the information, so it stuck.

What do you tell parents when they ask you about development? Is it what you really believe? There came a time when I defined what I truly believed about child development. Of course, it matched the current beliefs in the field of early learning, but I took ownership of it. It was my teachable moment. I needed to know, and I found my answers from books, from people I knew, and from experience.

When children can tell you what they need to know, can they be wrong? Jack knew he wanted to read more words. I waited for the punch line, and he told me what he was ready to learn. He told me what it was that I should teach him that day. So I did.

What will you teach today? How do you know it is the right thing?

Suggested Reading

Hewitt, Deborah. 1995. *So this is normal too? Teachers and parents working out developmental issues in young children.* Saint Paul: Redleaf Press.

15

Wet Socks Can Ruin Your Day

My just-washed socks aren't dry yet. They have been in the dryer for almost twenty minutes, but the towels are slowing down the drying process. Other socks in my sock drawer are thick and heavy. With the arrival of summer heat those socks will be uncomfortable all day. I decide that I will just wear my socks a little wet, and they will dry out eventually. It is a minor irritant, but irritating just the same.

So I go to work. I already feel icky because my feet are wet. To add another layer of annoyance, the person who closed my room last night forgot to vacuum. My feet feel icky, and my room feels icky. It doesn't have that fresh, ready-to-go feeling that I am used to in the morning. Normally I have such a great closer. She always leaves everything in its place, the chairs perfectly lined up at the tables. Then she sprays a scented air freshener when she leaves, so the room even smells sweet in the morning. Not today. Today the chairs are still stacked from the floor being somewhat mopped. Yesterday's art remains lie on the rug, and there is definitely no pretty scent. My feet are icky, the room is icky, and three parents just ran in and ran out as they dropped off the beginnings of my class for the day. Somehow, I don't feel ready for it all to begin.

"Miss Cindy." There is a tug on my pant leg as Jenna speaks, "Do you want to play pizza place this morning?"

"Thank you, but not right now, Jenna. I have to put the chairs out."

A little later: "Miss Cindy." She tugs again. "Do you want to play Candyland?"

"No, thank you. Maybe Jack will play with you." I vacuum.

"Miss Cindy." Tug, tug. "Do you want to see who can build the biggest tower?" "No, I need to wash down the tables."

"Miss Cindy, why are you so sad today?" I stop, stunned. I haven't used a sharp tone, nor have I been rude.

"What makes you think I am sad, Jenna?" I am curious about what has given me away.

"Your face. It says you are sad. You aren't mad, but you're not happy. You aren't tired, because you always wear your hair in a pony when you are tired. So I figure it must be sad. Do you want to talk about it? You always say it is better if we talk about it."

"Jenna, you are right. I am sad, and maybe a little annoyed. Miss Sarah always leaves my room so nice, and this morning it wasn't as nice as usual. And my favorite socks weren't dry in the dryer, so I am wearing them wet."

She starts to laugh. "Your socks are wet! That is why you are sad." She giggles between each word. Jenna has one of those infectious laughs. Even the kids across the room cannot resist. Soon we are all laughing at my wet socks. Some children would not think wet socks were a laughing matter, but Jenna does. She thinks it is ridiculous, even hilarious. She is right; it is ridiculous that I am so intensely affected by wet socks. In the scheme of the real world, even in a four-year-old's world, wet socks should not have enough power to ruin our whole morning.

I tell her how much better she makes me feel as we laugh at my wet socks, that she is a good friend to notice that I am sad and try to help me. How lucky I am to have her in my life! Then we cut sock shapes out of white paper and create our own silly socks. We hang them on a line to dry with a note that says, "Wet socks can't ruin my day!"

Teach Children to Be Good Friends

Strong relationships give us power to recognize the other person's mood. We can see that her face doesn't look happy or, in my case, that I was allowing silly circumstances to disrupt my ability to be present and aware of the children. But thankfully, they were present and aware of me. It was their turn to be the person who empowers. Jenna saw my displeasure and was using any tactic she knew to bring me to a better place. Relationships, given the room to grow and operate, are two-way exchanges. We give children our energy, our hearts, and our time every day. If we allow it to happen, relationships can refill our "give tanks" and lighten our hearts.

Jenna learned a lesson here as well. She learned that she knew how to be a good friend. Her input into my morning helped to brighten our day. She felt proud that she had done a good deed. Reinforcing children's positive impact on their world builds their self-esteem and confidence, ultimately empowering them to continue having a positive effect on their world.

Children begin to develop social competence from an early age. In the preschool class it is all about friendships. I cannot count the times that a preschool teacher will hear the sad statement "They don't like me anymore." Usually it is followed by "because they won't play with me" or "they won't do what I say" or any number of declarations of friendship trouble. Many times children simply need reassurance that just because their friend is playing with someone different doesn't mean that they are no longer friends. It just means that we can have more than one friend. The child who says, "You're not my friend anymore," needs help expressing hurt feelings in a more appropriate manner. For example: "That was not a nice thing to do" or "I don't like it when you hit me."

Preschool teachers lay the foundation for future friendships. We teach children how to be true to friends, how to set boundaries of friendship, and how to experience the rewards of a great friendship—as I did with Jenna.

There was a time when I had a friend whom I did not enjoy being around. She was a complainer. I met her when I was going through some rough personal times. As they say, "Birds of a feather flock together." So we got together and whined. She whined about her problems, and I sympathized—oh, so awful! Then I whined about my sorry life, and she empathized—oh, so awful! The difference was that I got up and changed my circumstances. I was motivated for change. She, on the other hand, enjoyed her misery. So she whined about her problems, and I no longer sympathized. I gave her encouragement and ideas about how she could make her life better. She gave me excuses. I rejoiced in my success, and she interrupted. The bright light that was shining in my life was more than she wanted to see. I spent less and less time with her.

Jacob was a master whiner. I tried every trick in the book—not this book but any other book I could find. I told him I couldn't understand him when he whined, and I refused to respond to his whiny words. The other children didn't even like to play with him, which resulted in more whining. We tried to define a nonwhiny voice versus a whiny voice. I tried tape-recording him and letting him listen to it (only him, of course). We tried puppets. We tried to get him to smile when he talked. Amazingly, this child could whine and smile at the same time. I told you he was a master whiner! He reminded me of my whining friend. I decided it was time for the cold, hard truth. So the next time he came to whine that nobody would play with him, I sat down. I put us eyeball-to-eyeball, looked at him straight, and said, "People do not like to hear people whine. The tone of voice is unpleasant. Kids like you; they just don't like it when you speak in a whiny voice. They want to hear what you have to say, but when you whine, they can't understand you. If you want them to play with you, stop whining, and speak with your nice voice." So he did.

I had always taught children indirectly about how to be a good friend. Use your words. Play in a cooperative manner. Et cetera. But I hadn't taught them in a direct manner. I decided to change my methods. Finding opportunities to define what a good friend is and describe what actions go with friendship was not hard. Every day I planned a good friend event. We might practice being good friends by holding the doors open for each other. On a different day, we would practice being good friends by letting someone else go first. This was a hard one! When someone got hurt, I would ask one of the hurt child's friends to help me make the child feel better. Of course, children couldn't administer first aid, but they could hold the hurt one's hand or get a tissue. Purposeful teaching of friendship was like healthy preventive medicine; it kept many potential problems at bay.

Reflection

Jenna's laugh brought me back to earth. Wet socks ruining an entire day is a ridiculous thought. My day was headed down the wrong path. If I had continued, I would have been miserable, taking several others with me. Many children can sense our moods; they know when we are in a funk. While it is difficult to be "up" and cheerful every moment of every day, we do our best. And on those days when our emotions sneak through, the children allow us to be us more than we allow ourselves. They are completely accepting of us; they look up to us. They adore us, even when our socks are wet.

Friendships are powerful. They have the ability to lift us up and tear us down. I often think about teaching children about how to be a good friend, yet I haven't spoken to one of my friends in months. I just never seem to find the time. Tending to our friendships as adults is just as important as building preschool friendships. Let's not forget our friends.

Teachers are more than friends. We provide systems, structure, and learning, but being a friend is an important part of teaching. Do you have "friend moments" with the children in your group? Are there times when you just enjoy being with them? Do you get to play Candyland? I have played more than 3,550 games of Candyland, most of which I have lost. In my last job I had my employers put in my contract that I was not expected to ever play Candyland again, but that other games would be provided. So we played other games. Do you play?

Some Friendship Teaching Goals

1. Plan responses to children's friendship statements. When statements like "They won't play with me" or "She doesn't like me anymore" come up, you will then have a plan of action, not just a quick empty answer like, "I am sure she still likes you." Share them with your classroom staff and parents; educate them as well.

2. Plan friendship activities. One of my favorites is to pair up children who don't usually play together and have them create something together. Then take a photo of their creation, and put it in a classroom book.

3. Dedicate a wall to the display of kind acts. When children exhibit a great friendship trait, make a note of it, and display it on the wall. You could note times when a child lets someone else go first or when a child helps another. You could include a drawing of a child helping a friend who fell down or even a simple act such as handing over a crayon.

Afterword

Have you ever lain on your back and watched the snow fall? If you haven't, you should try it. It is indescribable. Try it while you are young. I have found that as I grow older, it makes my head spin, and I get vertigo a bit. Anyway, there were about five of us watching the world from this angle when Jessie asked, "Why do the snowflakes come down in circles sometimes and sometimes they come straight?"

"I am not sure. What do you think?" I expected some type of interesting answer, but instead I got another question.

"What is 'think'?"

"Well, it's using your brain to process things. It sounds like talking to yourself inside your head."

We quietly watched the snow for a bit, and then Jarod asked, "How do you make the 'think' stop so you can just watch the snow again?"

I understand how he felt. Sometimes there is so much to think about when you are teaching that you want to quit thinking and just teach again. When I forget about all the things I have to do and just be myself—those are the best times. Always thinking about what to say, who is saying what and did I write it down, and don't forget to write it down later . . . All of that can get distracting and exhausting.

One day, I just relaxed and taught. It all began to come naturally. I knew what was best for children. I knew how to serve families. I knew how to create an optimal early learning environment. It all just became habit.

Now I can relax and enjoy it. I still challenge myself to go the extra mile, to create opportunities for curiosity, to include parents at a new level, and to teach to the individual. But every day, while I am teaching, I enjoy it.

We learn from our mistakes as well. We will try to teach something nobody is interested in. We will read a book that the children don't like. We will try to bake cookies, and they won't turn out. We will experience disappointment, rejection, sometimes public ridicule. We may know a child who battles a life-threatening illness. We may know a child who doesn't get to live the rest of her life. Our backs will ache, our brows will sweat, and our hearts will break.

But we will also know the power of a hug. We will have paintings of houses and flowers. We will stop illness with a wash of our hands, and we will listen to the birth of a new song. We will see purity. We will slow down to see nature perform miracles in new butterflies, melting snow, and seeds that rupture into life. We will be there to see a child discover knowledge. We will watch creativity create, thinking begin, and personalities become. Our bodies will become strong, our energies will be reenergized, and our hearts will love.

Every day you teach. What will you learn today?

APPENDIX A

Burnout Assessment Questionnaire

- In the morning when you wake up, are you excited to go to work, or are you looking for a way not to go?
- Did you recently avoid doing what you know is best for a child because you didn't have the energy?
- Have you overreacted in a situation, been irritable, or felt frustrated today?
- Have you had unexplained headaches or tension in your back, shoulders, or neck this week?
- Do you wake up tired?
- Have you taken time to enjoy yourself/family/hobbies/friends this week?
- Have you been bored at work?
- Do you feel unappreciated, or do you have trouble seeing why you value your work?

Discuss this questionnaire with a coworker or another person with whom you have a close relationship.

If you answered yes to any or many of these questions, determine the "why" behind each answer. If the conversation reveals that you have an overall dissatisfaction with your job, discuss it with your supervisor ASAP. Create a plan of action to rejuvenate yourself.

Remember

Caring for yourself is the best gift you can give those you love.

APPENDIX B

Individual Goal Chart

Name: _____

Activity and Day

1. _____

Done _____

2. _____

Done _____

Name: _____

Activity and Day

1. _____

Done _____

2. _____

Done _____

Name: _____

Activity and Day

1. _____

Done _____

2. _____

Done _____

Individual Goal Sheet

Name _____ Week of _____

Talent Area _____

Goal _____

_____

_____

_____

Specific activities in lesson plan to help achieve this goal:

Day: M T W Th F

Activity _____

Day: M T W Th F

Activity _____

NOTES

Works Cited

Bronfenbrenner, Urie. 1979. *The ecology of human development: Experiments by nature and design.* Cambridge, MA: Harvard University Press.

Copple, Carol, and Sue Bredekamp, eds. 2009. *Developmentally appropriate practice in early childhood programs serving children from birth through age 8,* 3rd ed. Washington, DC: National Association for the Education of Young Children.

Gardner, Howard. 2006. *Multiple intelligences: New horizons.* New York: BasicBooks.

Gartrell, Dan. 2006. *A guidance approach for the encouraging classroom.* 4th ed. Clifton Park, NY: Thompson Delmar Learning.

Jalongo, Mary Renck, and Joan P. Isenberg. 2000. *Exploring your role: A practitioner's introduction to early childhood education.* Upper Saddle River, NJ: Merrill.

Johnson, Jeff A. 2007. *Finding your smile again: A child care professional's guide to reducing stress and avoiding burnout.* Saint Paul: Redleaf Press.

Johnson, Spencer, M.D. 2003. *The present: The gift that makes you happy and successful at work and in life.* New York: Doubleday.

U.S. Department of Health and Human Services. 1992. *Caregivers of young children: Preventing and responding to child maltreatment.* User manual series. Child Welfare Information Gateway. http://www.childwelfare.gov/pubs/usermanuals/caregive/caregivec.cfm.